MOTELS

HOTELS

RESTAURANTS

AND BARS

MOTELS, HOTELS,

RESTAURANTS AND BARS

AN ARCHITECTURAL RECORD BOOK

PUBLISHED BY F. W. DODGE CORPORATION, NEW YORK

Copyright 1945, 1947, 1948, 1950, 1951,
1952, 1953 by F. W. Dodge Corporation

All rights reserved

This book or any part thereof must not
be reproduced in any form without the
written permission of the publisher.

PRINTED AND BOUND IN U. S. A.

DISCARDED
WIDENER UNIVERSIT

WIDENER COLLEGE
LIBRARY
CHESTER, PENNSYLVANIA
108883

CONTENTS

INTRODUCTION

What makes for success in a motel, hotel, restaurant or bar? Why do people stop and enter the Sunrise when they might choose the Sunset next door? Part of the answer to these questions is by nature managerial, but an equally important part is inherently physical. In this book our concern is with the significance of the design of the physical plant, and in showing the reader how good design can benefit both the owner and the public.

The text and illustrations were first published in Architectural Record on the two-fold basis that only architects possess the rounded training, technical know-how and artistic imagination necessary to make such buildings equally satisfying to both management and customer, and that competent and tasteful design pays off in increased profit to the owner. In making this volume available to both the general public and the design profession, the editors of Architectural Record hope that it will achieve three objectives. First, they hope that owners of motels, hotels, restaurants and bars who read these pages will be persuaded that a high level of design pays. Second, the editors hope prospective investors in such projects will realize the business wisdom of engaging professional architectural talent early in the game. Finally, we hope that architects will find this book a handy guide to contemporary examples of considerable merit.

In spite of generally increased public travel and the large volume of building going forward, we have only begun to meet the need for the kinds of buildings and facilities discussed here. Moreover, we are convinced the case for competent design will become better understood as competition increases.

If this volume helps bring about such an understanding and serves as an aid to architects, then it shall have served its purpose.

James S. Hornbeck

Senior Associate Editor
Architectural Record

Top left, *Tourist Court Journal;* Lower right, *Morley Baer*

MOTELS MOVE INTO THE SELECT CIRCLE

In the pages that follow it should be amply demonstrated that motor courts, or "motels," have reached the point of architectural importance. Moreover, it takes little reading between the lines to see that their impact reaches not only the city hotel but also the resort hotel. They might almost be said to represent a new way of vacation life.

Certainly the highway hotel has long since grown out of its early "Rooms for Tourists" or "Cabins for Rent" stages. In the sun-belt states — California, Arizona, Texas, Florida — the motel has become a full-blown resort hotel, complete with luxurious rooms, expensive restaurants, even bathing girls. There are swimming pools, tennis courts, private patios, room service, lounges, bars, and so on. Gone are the days, too, when the city hotel manager could scornfully say, "Only a certain type of people stay in those things." In short, motels are now big business.

To the architect, the significant thing in this cycle is that now the motels are entering his own purview. An article in a recent issue of *Tourist Court Journal* was entitled, "They Could Always be Used as Chicken Houses." From the days when the pioneer cabin builder fell back on this safety factor, the motel has left behind its era of back-yard design. It has also passed through its period of garish imitation and amateurish staginess. It now has its own stature, and is asserting it in a new architectural consciousness.

It is significant, too, that being a new industry the motel interests are far from hide-bound in matters of design. They are a modern American institution, alert to and sympathetic with contemporary manners.

As a new concept of vacation living, the motel runs to bright, gay informality, rather than the dull plush of the old front-porch hotels. Convenience is still the rule of the road, a rule being interpreted in ever-higher standards of services and appointments.

The gayety in such an architectural assignment, however, must be tempered with a thorough recognition of commercial matters of planning. The S.R.O. signs will not last forever. Neither will the motels likely settle into standard patterns, for the variations in type, extent of services, price and location will make each a highly individual problem, to tax the ingenuity of the architect not only in design but also in the handling of rather complicated economics.

CALIFORNIA HIDE-AWAY, MOTEL STYLE

Julius Shulman Photos

Town and Desert Apartments, Palm Springs, Calif.

H. W. Burns, Owner and Designer

I F the "motel" is the modern version of a hotel, this one is a similar model of an apartment hotel for a vacation spot. Its rooms are really small apartments, designed for Californians who can afford to get-away-from-it-all in elegant seclusion at Palm Springs. While the convenience and informality notes are clear, this is far removed from the roadside sleeping concept of the more typical motor courts. Its design contemplates a commune-with-nature type of holiday where a swim and a sun bath are the doctor's prescription.

Julius Shulman Photos

A little study of this plan is almost bound to impress one with the idea that here indeed is a new way of life, at least for those times when one craves a real rest. One gets interested, too, in the owner's way of life in this new concept of a building venture

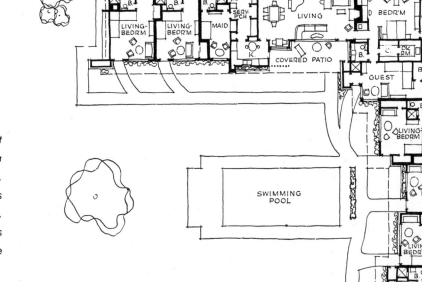

Each unit has a small Pullman-type
kitchen, lightly screened off when in use,
completely hidden by louvered doors at
other hours. Note air conditioning duct

Julius Shulman Photos

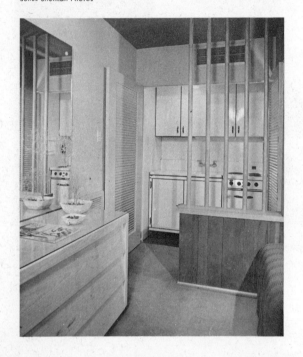

The broader view of the typical rental unit, below, shows daybeds in a hotel-type placement in the combination living-bedroom
fashion, complete even to the built-in radio in the corner

Outdoor and indoor space merge so completely that in these photographs it is difficult to find the line of enclosure. Views through the glass wall are from the owner's living room toward covered patio. Note same brick inside and out

VACATION HOTEL IN THE MOTEL MANNER

Morley Baer Photos

Carmel Valley Inn, Monterey County, California

Robert R. Jones, Architect

A COMPELLING example of the "motel" grown to the stature of a resort institution, this one has the spread that typifies California relaxation. It was this "spread" that dictated the low, dispersed arrangement, done in the ranch tradition. The angling wings give each unit a little patio, and also leave the possibility of extending wings in the future. The views, both natural and man-made, provided another design theme, which was carried out with a maximum of glass to bring the outside inward on every possible location. This was one factor in the use of covered porches rather than interior halls; glazing can always be put between the porch posts if it seems desirable, without blocking off views of the mountains or of the swimming pool and gardens.

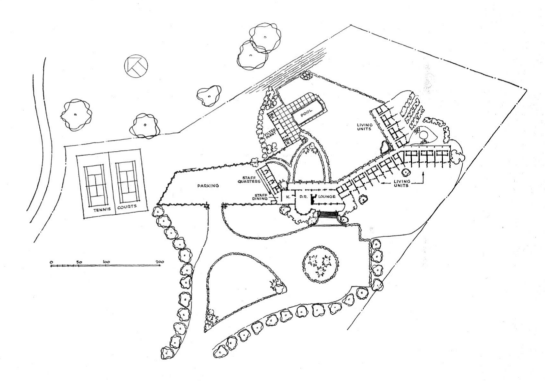

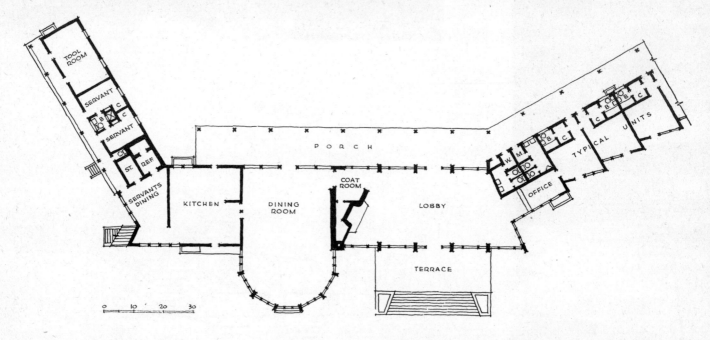

Morley Baer Photos

Lobby and dining room facilities, with the kitchen area, were made oversize to allow for a future expansion to 40 or 60 rooms. The public area, with its lounge porch, was placed for views both front and rear. Service wing was turned to provide a windscreen

The architect mentions that cost considerations dictated many changes, including elimination of a massive chalkrock fireplace and furnace flue form, in favor of redwood covered brick flues. Perhaps the result in the photograph above is not properly in the ranch tradition, but it is doubtful if the guests would be moved to anything but hearty approval

An eye more knowing than that of the average guest might notice that the rooms follow an idea successfully used in modern hotels — wide, shallow rooms, daybeds, scaled down furniture for an atmosphere of spaciousness

While the distant views are fully up to the California standard, the foreground is not forgotten. Nevertheless, eye-catchers are low enough for distant vision

Morley Baer Photos

No scaling down of furniture is seen in this view, though it is still there. Glass walls on the porch side inescapably draw the eye of anybody in the room until the porch area is effectively added to that of the room

A MULTI-SERVICE MOTEL AT SANTA MONICA

Julius Shulman Photo

Carl's Sea Air, Roosevelt Highway, Santa Monica, Calif.

Burton A. Schutt, Architect

Accustomed as this architect is to handling problems of income production, he was confronted with an unusual list of them here, for this motel extends a wide variety of highway services to motorists along the bustling Roosevelt Highway, paralleling the Pacific. There is auto service, food service to cars, table service in a dining room, cocktail bar and rooms of the motel type. The site, on the far side of the road from the beach, introduced its own difficulties. The result is an elevated building, to keep highway traffic from obstructing the view, with rooms angled on the plan so that each faces the sea. The dispositions follow in general the natural lines of the palisades behind, with public areas close to the road, sleeping rooms recessed in a deep V.

Bedrooms are elevated to get a view of the sea across the highway, and are staggered to face that view. Triangular spaces left are utilized in the rear for closets and baths, on the front for little private balconies. The architect calls particular attention to the arrangement of corner windows, in a manner designed to trap all breezes as desired. Rear balcony gives access to sleeping rooms

Julius Shulman Photos

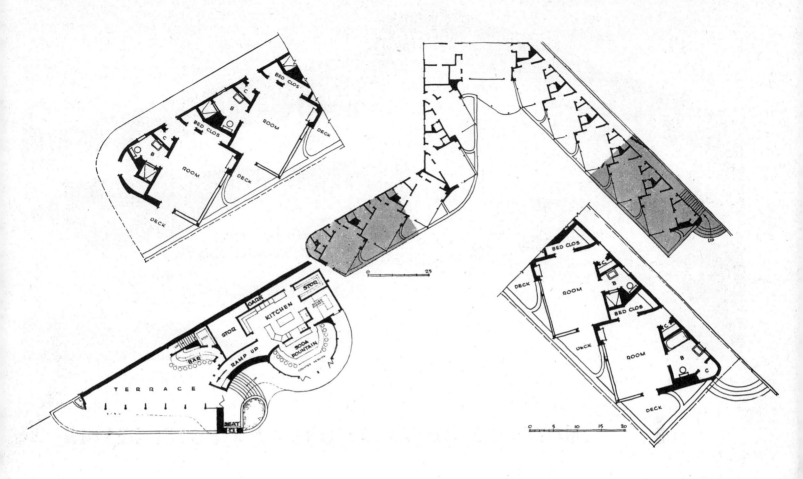

Space below raised sleeping floor is utilized for garage. Garage is of concrete construction, for fire protection, construction above is frame and stucco. In the plan above, note different levels of soda fountain, kitchen and terrace, the last elevated for view. Stairs at back of bar lead to lounge rooms and storage spaces on the second floor

MOTEL ACCOMMODATIONS IN A HOTEL DESIGN

Tropic Palms Hotel, Wilshire Boulevard, West Los Angeles

Burton A. Schutt, Architect

Julius Shulman Photos

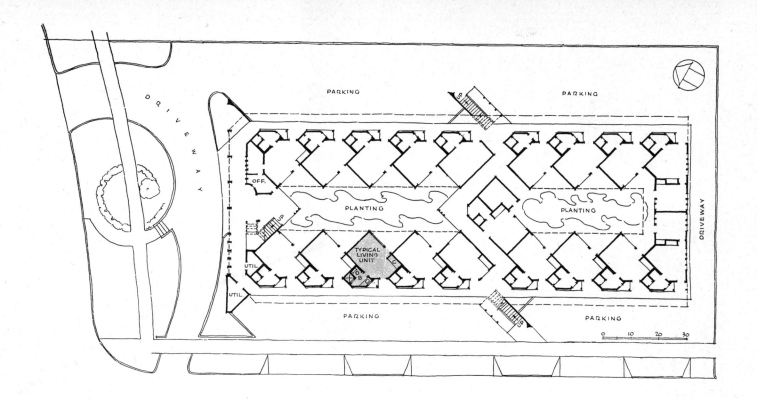

WHILE a motel seems to imply a large open site, this one had to be accommodated on a lot 100 by 200 ft. Thus it comprises motel-type units put together in a hotel design. And the architect was primarily occupied with income matters, not with any *tour de force* in architectural design. In this latter respect he was further handicapped by materials shortages, as this hotel was built before the close of the war. In any case, Tropic Palms, designed to offer middle-class accommodations on busy Wilshire Boulevard, has been exceedingly popular, and has enjoyed the income of a luxury hotel. Setting the rooms into the plan at a 45° angle brought light and privacy that would not otherwise be possible. Entrances from the outside balconies have proved to be quite satisfactory, particularly as to maintenance. Eventually plantings will give a hanging garden effect.

Parking spaces encircling the building, combined with outside entrances opening directly to the parking areas, have preserved the convenience and informality of motel accommodations

While the angling of individual units may have narrowed the interior court, it gives each apartment a great deal more privacy than would be possible with any other placing, and each gets a private balcony. The design contemplates plantings on the balconies, to soften the straight lines in a hanging garden effect

Julius Shulman Photos

Interiors are simply designed and simply furnished, but a bold use of art forms in sculptures, paintings and furnishings lifts the rooms beyond the impersonality and monotony so commonly associated with hotel rooms

carousel

Julius Shulman Photos

LOOK LIKE HOME

Richard Massen

and Roland Greene

Owners and Designers

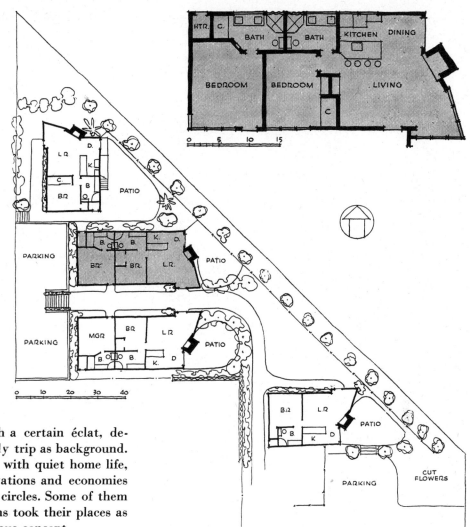

Two G.I.'s, tackling civilian life with a certain éclat, designed their own motel, with a study trip as background. Their theme was a zip *not* associated with quiet home life, which shows in extemporaneous innovations and economies thoroughly acceptable in architectural circles. Some of them which started as shortage substitutions took their places as perfectly logical items in the adventurous concept.

Cottage type units were economically built. For example, fixed window sash were designed for a standard glass size bought in case lots. Windows are fixed since no opening hardware was available at time of construction (top and bottom louvers give ventilation)

Julius Shulman Photos

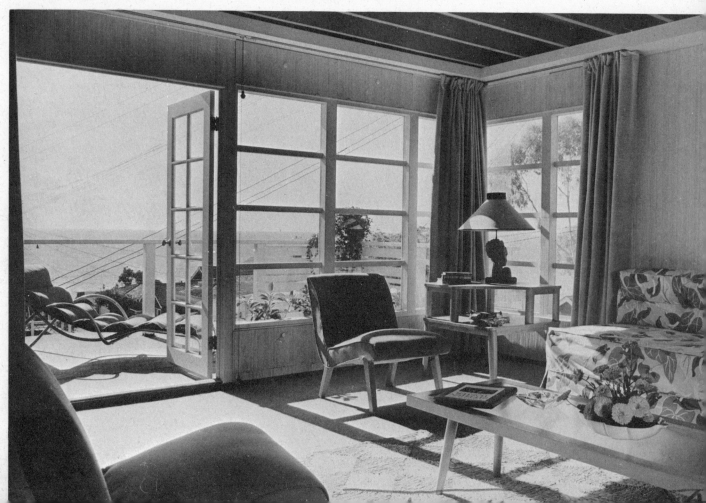

22

Simple materials boldly used carry out the designers' theme of not-like-home innovations, as for example the Lally column, the plain fireplace wall, fluorescent light fixtures used as drapery hangers, the simple if rather oddly assorted furnishings. The economy tenet of design did not, however, prevent such comfort items as radiant heated floors, and infrared heat lamps in bathrooms. Colors are also on the thematic note — gay yellow and cerise accents on gray

prepared by
Frederic Arden Pawley, Architect

This comprehensive study of the architectural requirements of a multi-million-dollar industry was undertaken by Mr. Pawley at the joint request of Architectural Record and Hotel Management, in which it also appears. This editorial collaboration has made it possible to assemble in one place information from a diversity of sources. Unifying the data obtained from both architects and motel operators should help each to appreciate the value of the other's training and experience

Julius Shulman

INTRODUCTION

Someone has said that the motor court was sired by the tourist cabin and dammed by the hotel. The offspring is now considered a legitimate get of an economic trend and the transportation-accommodation preference of the American public. These tendencies are here examined in detail as a basis for architectural planning and as promotional background for architects interested in this $750,000,000 business (estimate copyright *Tourist Court Journal*). Recognition of needs of motorists and of the automobile as a planning unit are basic appeals of the motor court. As in colonial days, today's roadside inns, spaced at convenient day's journeys from each other, provide lodging, food and protection.

The hotel, a result of urban and resort concentrations, of development of railroad and elevator, and of the concept of superior service to guests, became a vertical structure for many urban reasons. It fell into a deep financial hole after the overbuilding boom of

1922–29 from which over 80 per cent of the nation's hotels emerged by way of bankruptcy, foreclosure and reorganization. Ten years later New York City still had many empty hotel rooms despite a two-year World's Fair. An occupancy of 70 per cent room capacity meant a going business, however, because operating costs were still depressed. World War II sent hotel occupancy to 93 per cent and raised operation expenses; the break-even point is now as high as 85 per cent occupancy. Occupancy for the country as a whole for 1948 was 86 per cent, for half of 1949, 84 per cent. Average "sale per occupied room" (room revenue or rate) is higher than it has ever been, reflecting increased costs of hotel operation. Charts on next two pages show these trends. growth of motor hotel idea and important underlying travel statistics.

Motor courts, a depression-sown industry, sprang up in abundance in the 30's as tourist cabins. Many are the euphemisms for their most profitable kind of busi-

Julius Shulman

Examples abound all over the U. S.: top row left, Skyline Motor Hotel, Front Royal, Va.; center, Pepper Tree Inn, Palm Springs, Calif., Stewart Williams, Archt.; right, Return Motor Court, New Market, Va., Clarence W. Wenger, Archt.

Pawley

Julius Shulman

Bottom left, Palm Springs Biltmore, Palm Springs, Calif., Frederick Monhoff, Archt.; center, Contentment House, Desert Hot Springs, Calif., John Lautner, Archt.

ness. We hear of one which turned away any travelers with luggage on Saturdays and Sundays. Conditions were so bad that in 1940 the Chief of the FBI published a popular magazine article tracing a number of crimes in lurid detail to tourist camps. (14) This blast forced a better element of operators to associate and in self-protection to develop standards of management policy, equipment, specifications and sanctions against offending members. Inspection and listing by Duncan Hines and the A.A.A. have also come to indicate acceptability. Elmer Jenkins, A.A.A. National Touring Director, states that of approximately 30,000 motor courts in the country their Accommodations Directory (131) lists only 3522 (about 1 in 12) and that only about 1 in 30 is recommended without qualifications. From a quick check it would appear that about 1 in 100 has architectural interest or planned efficiency.

The reason for this is not only Topsy-growth, but also development of planning, construction and finish specifications by lay associations of operators. A 1946 survey indicated that 18 per cent of courts reporting employed architects. Investments in motor court construction are by no means beneath an architect's notice. *Tourist Court Journal* (128) recommended in 1940 that no new court be built for less than $50,000. In 1948 the *average* investment, for the country as a whole, including land and equipment, was about $70,000 (average 20 rental units). The U. S. Department of Commerce Small Business Manual on motor courts (9) recommended (1945) a size of 35 to 50 rental units, with 10 units an absolute minimum. Costs per unit, completely furnished, are now between $3500 and $5000, but horizontal construction is estimated at $\frac{1}{3}$ of vertical. City hotel costs per room are $12,000 to $24,000, including full hotel facilities.

The industry sells a fugitive product. "At the end of a day's operation, any room not sold is a piece of merchandise that has perished . . . revenue . . . has

MOTELS

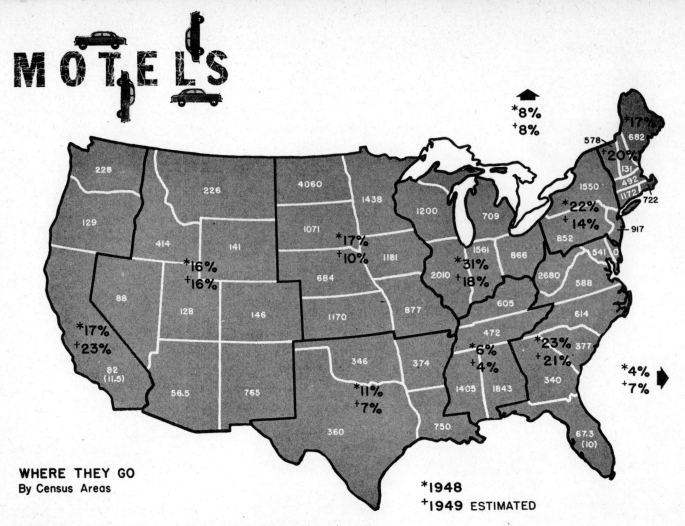

*8%
+8%

*17%

578
682

*20%
131
492
1172
722

1550
*22%
+14%
852
917
541 0

*17%
+10%
1181
866
588

*16%
+16%
684
2680
614

*31%
+18%
2010
605

*17%
+23%
146
877
472
*23%
+21%
377

128
1170
*6%
+4%
340

88
346
374
*4%
+7%

82
(11.5)
56.5
765
*11%
+7%
1405
1843

360
750
67.3
(10)

228
226
4060
1438
1200
709
1561

129
414
141
1071

WHERE THEY GO
By Census Areas

*1948
+1949 ESTIMATED

Small figures show motel density (ratio, total rural surfaced highway mileage to number motels listed by A.A.A. — and for Fla. and Calif., total courts). Large figures: where vacation travelers go

HOW FAR VACATION TRAVELERS GO

TRIP DISTANCE	ACTUAL 1948	ESTIMATE 1949
<500 MILES	20%	13%
500–1000	22	17
1000–1500	16	13
1500–2500	19	23
>2500	23	34

VACATION TRAVEL

43% OF MEN REPLYING TOOK OVERNIGHT BUSINESS TRIPS (AV. 9 TRIPS EACH IN 1948)

by
AUTO ▓▓▓▓▓▓▓▓ 73%
RAIL ▭ 43%
AIR ▭ 25%
BUS ▭ 12%
OTHER ▯ 2%

SOME REPORTED MORE THAN ONE METHOD OF TRAVEL

BUSINESS TRIPS

1945
83   65   40

AUTO
RAIL   AIR   BUS

1947
77   55   32

1948
84   71   50

<200 MILES   200–500   500–1000

TRANSPORTATION PREFERENCE

been lost forever." (9) Every effort must be made to keep occupancy high. The architect can help in this by providing the sales appeal of good design and planning, which the operator has approached only in a tentative, inexperienced fashion.

Extravagant claims concerning the number of chain motor court operations already planned and ready for construction have not materialized. Motor hotel profits are high for a hard-working husband-and-wife team of owner-managers (nationwide average net profit 29 per cent for 1948, equal to 9.6 per cent on investment). Mr. Louis Toth of Horwath & Horwath, Hotel Accountants, reports, on the basis of a number of studies, that chain operation will not work — that the owner must be present daily. Long hours, temptation to relax stand-

ards, possibility of organized 3-shift labor, militate against a chain, non-resident-owner operation. The obvious answer would appear to be Howard Johnson or oil-company-filling-station franchise type of organization with profit-sharing owners-managers associated for mass buying, advertising, financing, etc. As far as can be ascertained such an operation of any considerable size does not yet exist in this field.

Proposals have been made to create a series of satellite motor hotels around a main city hotel, tied in with switchboard and other services. Intent was for outlying units to feed guests to the central hotel and take overflow. Result in one case tried was reversed flow! Guests too late to stay in motor hotel went reluctantly to big hotel, where they had to buck all the vexatious prob-

Travel data on this page from American Magazine, "1948 Travelogue".

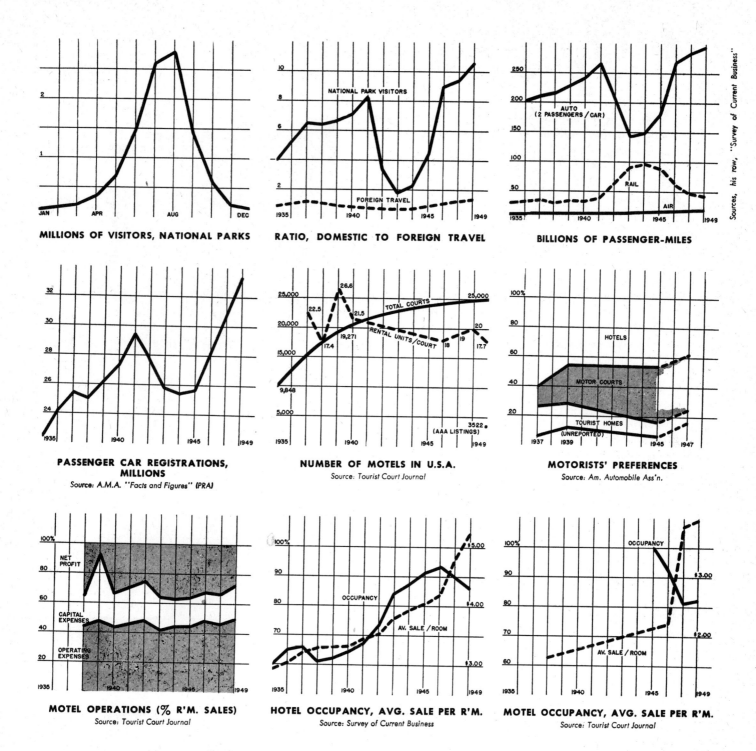

MILLIONS OF VISITORS, NATIONAL PARKS

RATIO, DOMESTIC TO FOREIGN TRAVEL

BILLIONS OF PASSENGER-MILES

PASSENGER CAR REGISTRATIONS,
MILLIONS
Source: A.M.A. "Facts and Figures" (PRA)

NUMBER OF MOTELS IN U.S.A.
Source: Tourist Court Journal

MOTORISTS' PREFERENCES
Source: Am. Automobile Ass'n.

MOTEL OPERATIONS (% R'M. SALES)
Source: Tourist Court Journal

HOTEL OCCUPANCY, AVG. SALE PER R'M.
Source: Survey of Current Business

MOTEL OCCUPANCY, AVG. SALE PER R'M.
Source: Tourist Court Journal

lems which the motor hotel solves: heavy traffic, parking trouble, car storage charges, the luggage dilemma, tips in and out, the parade of tired and wrinkled family through a busy, critical lobby, city noise and city atmosphere. (36) A hotel accountant executive on a trip to Florida with suites available to him without cost at leading hotels found his tips and other expenses made paying his way in motor courts (with newer furniture) less expensive than accepting the free hotel accommodations.

A year ago the American Hotel Association made an extensive survey of roadside housing, parts of which were condensed into a booklet, "How to Sell the Motor Traveler" (1). Many constructive suggestions were made and a number of hotels have now recognized the automobile by providing motor lobbies and special services. A feud of considerable heat has been waged by the motor court trade papers. The recommendation, based on this survey, that the hotels should get into the motor court business, and publication of a number of motor courts in architectural and hotel periodicals, resulted in a flamboyant headline, "Lo, How Have the Mighty Fallen!" (32) in one motor court magazine. Apparently its editors were not aware that, some years earlier, architects had advocated a building type combining some hotel facilities with special motorists' accommodations. These Highway Hotels, Outpost Inns or Motor Hotels are a more impressive expression of the idea, which is as old as the early Federal hotels and later resort centers. A danger is latent: if the operation takes

MOTELS

on too many of the hotel's traditional services, functions and maintenance problems, operating costs mount and the situation becomes circular and vicious.

Restaurant service is not agreed upon in the motor court industry (18.3 per cent have coffee rooms; *Tourist Court Journal*, 1946). One deluxe Western court in a suitable location reports food and drink revenue three times that from rentals. It is agreed that no one should start a food operation in connection with a motor court without experienced management. Filling stations are also not considered desirable unless isolation demands them (25 per cent; *Tourist Court Journal*, 1946). National statistics show a very gradual growth of motor court income from these other sources of revenue except in the North Central states, where they gained in 1948 at the expense of room rentals.

●

The following program notes can be used as a check list by an architect designing a motor court or motor hotel and will be found to contain suggestions for all parts of the project. They are based on recommendations of a number of architects, experienced operators, travel executives and travelers. Certain operational items (not requiring architectural provisions) have been included to indicate the scope of services and conveniences offered by some installations.

LOCATION, SITE, PLOT PLAN

Since all business comes from the highway, selection of location and site is of first importance. Site treatment is no less important, because the basic appeal of the motor court is its recognition of the automobile as a controlling factor. Plot plans therefore deserve careful study.

Relation to automobile travel: Location must consider loci of average day's rides (200–400 miles) from other stops on natural touring routes to national parks, resort areas and other vacation regions.

Relation to town or city: Availability of: employees, fuel, water, electricity, gas, sewer, laundry service.

Proximity to restaurants & service stations (if not provided).

Traveling salesmen visiting town or city are often important year-round, repeating source of business.

If a restaurant is provided, the nearby town or city must also be considered as a source of food, supplies, waste disposal and local business.

Availability of taxicabs may affect local business.

Relation to highway: First step in considering locations is to study current federal, state, local highway and traffic planning programs.

Secure passenger-traffic car counts.

Julius Shulman

Site plan of Palm Springs Biltmore, Palm Springs, Calif. (Frederick Monhoff, Archt.) is evident in air view. This type of facility, with swimming pool, restaurant, lounges, etc., and in resort country, is increasingly used for stops longer than overnight. Indeed, many motels are built for exactly this purpose

MOTELS

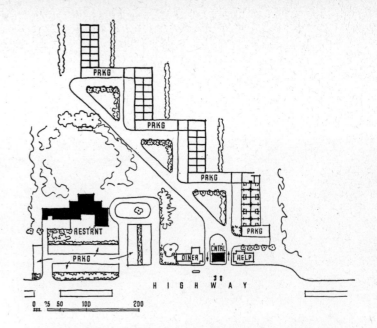

Two examples of site planning for multiple-unit motels (David Fried, Archt.): above, 12-unit buildings each with utility room; common parking for each building, not usually considered as satisfactory as individual car parking at each unit. Opposite page: four-unit buildings each with central utility core, parking at each unit's door. In both examples, "front office" control is at highway entrance. Restaurant, gas station, etc., are independent of motel proper, though somewhat related. Photos: top, attractive landscaping, Motel Robert, Christiansburg, Va. (Stone & Thompson, Archts.); below, light paving reflects glare, heat, shows dirt

Site should be on righthand side of highway going toward city unless on bypass.

Frontage on highway and sight distance for motorist are important factors in stopping cars. Minimum frontage should be 500 ft; 800 to 1000 ft is preferred. Car going 60 mph will stop comfortably in about 400 ft (40 mph, 200 ft).

Access driveway must be easy from either side of highway.

If a dual road exists or is planned, proper authorities must be consulted to make certain of island crossovers.

Rake of highway headlights across site must be considered.

Avoid sites near hills. Grades create stopping and noise problems (up or down).

Site: Select fairly level ground to avoid expensive grading, foundation, driveway construction.

Good natural drainage is highly desirable.

Natural features are valuable: trees, water, views.

Consider orientation, microclimatology: sunlight, prevailing winds, lay of land.

Avoid location near other motor courts. Check zoning, ownership, availability, plans of owners of adjacent property. Motor courts do not thrive on competition. Consider acquisition of land to prevent competition and undesirable neighbors.

Driveways, parking: Stabilized or hard-surfaced driveways and parking areas minimize noise, dust (affects room maintenance).

Blacktop decreases sunlight glare and bad appearance of oil drippings.

Plan driveways and parking for: operation, appearance. (1) Route first to office (local temporary parking), then to parking, carports or garages related to rental units, finally to exit. (2) Curved alignments, staggered setbacks, angular placement of buildings can be planned to increase privacy and improve building orientation as well as to break up rigidity of traditional rectangular "tourist court" plot plan.

Check access to, curvature, grades of all driveways by driving over them before final construction. Plan driveways to avoid rake of car headlights across bedroom windows.

Decision on type of parking is basic: (1) outdoor (acceptable unless extreme climate); (2) carports; (3) garages.

Locate parking as near rental unit as possible.

Landscaping: Project must appeal to motorist from highway. Trees, shrubs, flowers, lawns, a stream or pond, every natural feature, should be exploited for its attraction value and made easy and economical to maintain in good condition. Landscaping can also afford

windbreaks, some degree of noise screening, shade, backgrounds, and can cut off undesirable views.

Local and regional planting varieties and schedules, required amount and availability of water for use on grounds, help for maintenance, planning and details to facilitate maintenance are all factors which in a larger-scale project indicate desirability of retaining a landscape architect, at least as a consultant.

Garden furniture should be chosen for durability and resistance to exposure. It should be painted light colors if used in evening. Steps, railings and lights may be required. Paved walks will reduce dirt carried into rooms.

GENERAL PLANNING; BASIC FACTORS

Number of rental units, employees: Usual initial motor court construction is 10–20 rental units. Husband-and-wife team can handle not more than about 12 units without extra help. Latest national average (*Tourist Court Journal*) is 17.7 units. Usual allowance is one maid to 10 rooms.

Provision for expansion: Many motor courts are built with expansion in mind and it is undoubtedly wise to underbuild (but not less than 10 units). Expansion is almost invariably horizontal, by additional structures rather than by additions to existing buildings, except

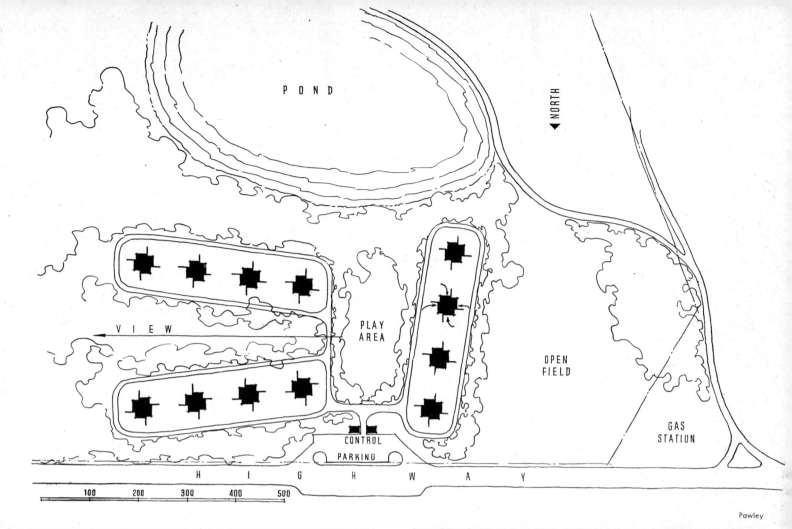

POND

NORTH

VIEW

PLAY AREA

OPEN FIELD

GAS STATION

CONTROL PARKING

H I G H W A Y

100 200 300 400 500

Pawley

restaurants. There are few two-story courts in spite of possible construction and maintenance economies. Unfortunately, an ultimate plan is rarely visualized at the start, and final results are often crowded, with poor access or other bad relationships. Some of the older installations show a great variety of rental unit types; improvements were made when newer units were built.

Flexibility, Variety: Flexibility of the rental unit plan is important and will be discussed later. In general, one may provide for alternate expansion areas and multiple uses of common facilities such as lounges, recreation or dining spaces. Another type of flexibility is involved in off-season closing of certain units — a good argument, where seasonal volume varies, for dividing total number of rental units into groups of 4, 6 or 8 to a building with separate utilities or cut-offs for each building. (Even-numbered groups preferred for backing up adjacent plumbing.) Variety will occur automatically in any adequately landscaped site. Attempts to achieve it by "architectural" or stylistic methods are soon dated and lose interest. In addition, the maintenance burden is increased in direct proportion to embellishment.

Combined or Separate Structures: Often the owner-manager's quarters are in a typical rental unit in the first stage of a small operation. A more developed type will provide an apartment with cooking and dining

M O T E L S

Pawley

Pawley

Maynard Parker

Pawley

Typical rental units: top, Princess Anne Motor Lodge, Williamsburg, Va.; left, El Rancho Motel, St. Albans, W. Va. (Robert Martens, Archt.); center, Tucson Biltmore, Tucson, Ariz.; right, Skyline Motor Hotel, Front Royal, Va.

facilities and private garage. This may be buffered from rental units by service spaces such as linen and utility rooms.

Individual cottages are more expensive to build than rows (unless terrain is uneven) and may give an unsubstantial appearance compared with 4, 6 or 8 unit buildings which provide more imposing architectural masses.

Circulation: Seasonal or weather considerations will affect planning of circulation. Covered access to rooms is desirable for guests and maids. Avoid changes in levels, if possible, to facilitate servicing and guest access. Some plans have covered circulation on one side and private covered terraces on the other.

Carports, Garages or Outdoor Parking; Dining Facilities; Service Station: All these basic factors should be considered in the preliminary general planning and provided for or discarded at the outset, unless the site is large enough to permit later decisions.

MAIN BUILDING; RENTAL OPERATIONS

Covered drive at office: For protection of guests; for discouraging trucks (low marquees used for same purpose by some service stations).

Lobby: For guest registration, rent payment, information, waiting, convenience sales. "Front desk" may be a small writing surface or can be dispensed with entirely if someone is always available to take care of guests at their cars. Registration card can be filled out and rent payment made in rental unit.

Office: For key-rack, safety deposit box, bookkeeping, purchasing, publicity, etc. Keys are best kept in locked cabinet (one standard visible key control system has considerable variety and capacity of equipment: wall cabinets, file drawers and hinged panels).

Supervision: Careful planning can make manager's locations oversee many functions of operation and save considerable time and effort in supervision.

Lounge: Newer courts are providing some common space where guests may gather, if they wish (particularly in bad weather), for social purposes, reading, letter-writing, waiting. It should have comfortable, durable furnishings, good lighting, homelike character; may have radio, television, bridge tables, desks, gift shop and wall maps.

Public toilets: For larger projects, highway hotels, inns.

Robert Cleveland

Front offices: top, Santa Ynez Inn, Los Angeles, Calif. (Alfred Gilman, Archt.); left, Tucson Biltmore; center, Palm Springs Biltmore; right, Return Motor Court, New Market, Va.

Julius Shulman

Maynard Parker

Pawley

Telephone booth(s): Particularly important if bid is being made for traveling salesmen (considered very desirable by some because of off-season and repeating volume).

Booth(s) should be oversize, have comfortable chair, large writing space, good light, fan, local and regional maps under glass, convenient telephone books.

Telephone switchboard: Complete telephone service throughout rental units is too expensive for many courts to consider. Some have intercommunication wall units which can be used two-way between main desk and guest room. This requires a switchboard and operator. Guests feel safer with communication service.

Service quarters: If project is isolated some employees may live on job. If not, locker rooms and toilets will be required. Check state labor laws for other requirements.

HOUSEKEEPING OPERATIONS, MAINTENANCE

Procedure and operation of housekeeping department varies from one installation to another; quantities, etc., (from which architect can develop room areas and equipment) must be decided upon by owner. Following notes give general data.

Linen: Operators are agreed on desirability of a central linen storage room under strict supervision. Four "turns" of linen are not enough to carry over a holiday weekend unless laundry service is better than average. This means shelf storage provision for *three* sets of everything changed daily: 1 set in room in use; 3 on shelf; 1 in laundry. In projects requiring several maids provide local, locked linen and room supplies closets for each maid. These may require spaces for:

sheets	bath mats	writing materials
pillow cases	soap	postcards
face towels	tissues	paper cups
bath towels	matches	sterilized glasses

Housekeeping storage: Cots or rolling utility beds (latter are about 18 by 40 by 46 in. high; mattresses; pillows.

Service closets, etc.: For cleaning equipment and supplies; floor maintenance appliances; slop sinks. For larger projects consider specially designed maids' carts with shelves and racks for: linen and room supplies, cleaning supplies, equipment.

Maintenance shops: For minor repairs and maintenance: Electrical; plumbing and heating; painting and

MOTELS

glazing. In extensive projects a Jeep or small truck can be equipped as a mobile repair unit.

Storage: For grounds equipment (mowers, hand tools, ladders, snow plow(s), shovels); garden furniture (winter storage); recreational equipment.

Fire protection: Insurance rates can be improved by careful consideration of fire protective measures throughout the project.

RENTAL UNITS

Identification of unit: Since motorists may arrive late, or may return to room late, building and unit identification should be provided. Buildings may be designated by letters, which should be prominently displayed, and rooms numbered as usual in hotels. Self-luminous letters and numbers may avoid necessity for insect-attracting, neighbor-annoying porch lights.

General planning and flexibility: Current trend is to make all rooms large enough for two double beds whether furnished that way or not. If traveling salesmen are an important part of the business, single rooms may be provided; but if so, they should be large enough for refurnishing as doubles.

Corner rooms may be made large, provided with double interconnecting doors for use *en suite* with adjacent room and rented at a premium. Suites may also be arranged with an entry shared by two rental units which becomes a private hall when they are rented together. Door-swings, including screen doors, must be considered to permit access for utility beds. One motor hotel is so planned that adjacent rental units, with such a joint entry, may be converted to three-room housekeeping apartments in times of changing business (due to depression or housing shortage).

Acceptable double-room sizes range from 14 by 14 to 16 by 18 ft. These are considerably larger than city hotel double rooms and give the motor court another selling point.

Housekeeping is easier and quicker if beds touch walls at heads only and if radiation is recessed.

Closets: Since 90–95 per cent of business is one-night, some new courts are installing inconspicuous hookstrips and dispensing with closets, or leaving off closet doors, not only to save money but to minimize tendency to leave articles in closed closets. Standard carpenter construction of closets with full door frame, door and trim begins to look more and more ridiculous. Very simple and inexpensive metal sliding doors are available which make full closet width accessible (half at a time). "Storagewall" treatment between rental units will not be satisfactory from sound reduction standpoint.

Contentment House, at Bubbling Well, Desert Hot Springs, Calif. (John Lautner, Archt.), is another motel-resort-cottage group. Each motor-apartment has a private garden, is protected from the surrounding desert, and has a complete kitchen. For relaxation there are hot and cold mineral baths; Palm Springs is six miles away

Julius Shulman

MOTELS

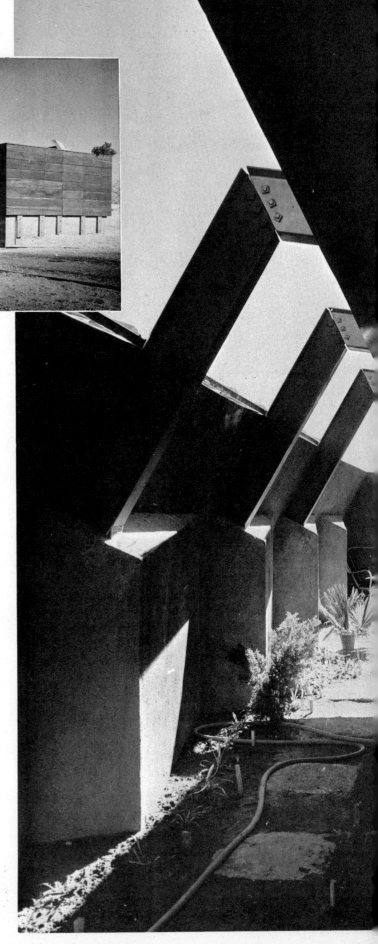

Contentment House: above, exterior of typical apartment, completely furnished, with car parking space alongside; below, interior, kitchen at far end; right, looking toward an apartment's private terrace

Julius Shulman

Windows: Metal casements seem to be preferred, with aluminum recommended to save painting (avoid flimsy sections). Projected sash and glass block panels with casement vents have also been used. Projected sash may give protection from weather and prowlers. Glass block affords protection, privacy, insulation, light distribution and reduces dust infiltration. Fixed glass (double-glazed where required), with screened louvers which can be shut, make a good arrangement where glass is accessible for washing outside. At least one set of louvers in each room should be easily opened from inside for fire escape hatchway.

One motor court problem when there is insufficient shelter from eaves, window hoods or porches, is the closing of rental unit windows in event of a sudden storm. Some method of closing from outside is desirable to avoid having to run in and out of every room.

Slate window stools make an attractive, easily cleaned, alcohol- and cigarette-proof detail. Screens are a must. Aluminum or other non-ferrous metal will save painting. Venetian blinds, with or without draperies, are considered essential for privacy and maximum ventilation; most recent courts have metal blinds. Venetian blinds are always difficult to clean and absorb and re-radiate solar heat inside the room, but there is at present no inexpensive substitute for the light control, privacy and ventilation they provide.

Awnings of light metal, with overlapping members spaced to permit better ventilation, are found in some courts. There is a tendency to paint alternate strips contrasting colors which makes a pattern of stripes too bold for many facade designs.

Doors: Screen doors may also be aluminum to save painting.

Keying of locks for various classes of entry is important:

Manager:	Grand Master Key
Maintenance:	Master key for all storage, shops, padlocks, slop sink closets.
Maids:	Master key for all rental units (keyed different from closets and garage doors) in each one-maid area with local linen closet subject to that master key and manager's Grand Master only. Maids' keys to be turned in each day.
Guests:	Rental units, closets and garage doors keyed alike.
Restaurant and Service Station:	On individual keys subject to manager's Grand Master only. (May be run as concessions.)

Oversize key tags should have post office box number rather than name and address.

When garages are provided, a door directly into the bedroom is convenient for luggage handling. Check insurance regulations. Some plans have door near rear of car, or to entrance porch or terrace. Overhead doors are found in most motor court garages.

 MOTELS

Porches, terraces: Some place to sit outdoors, with or without privacy, is appreciated by average motor-tourist. The building often has a continuous porch which affords circulation protected from weather for guests and maids. Some of the quite old examples link buildings by covered passages as well. Porches need not be wide. Six feet will permit passing behind furniture. Avoid wooden porch floors. Wear and repainting will make them more expensive eventually than more durable terrace materials.

Ceilings: Some examples have acoustic board ceilings which add somewhat to thermal insulation. Reduction of sound at source by acoustic absorption is first line of defense against noise.

Trim: Asphalt tile cove base is neat, durable and requires no paint. Narrow, flush metal door and window trim reduces maintenance and gives desirable simplicity. Door jamb trim should project far enough to receive molded base.

Colors: Variegated floors will show wear and dust less than plain colors. Tesselated patterns of quietly contrasting colors are found most practical. Wall colors should be selected to balance daylight effects. Rooms without sun may be made more cheerful by using

Plan types: top, single unit, prefabricated, The Inn, Bethlehem, N. H. (Dan Kiley, Archt.); below, double unit for use alone or as part of a 4-unit, Lovett's Cottages, Franconia, N. H.; right, 4 rooms around central core, Saltboxes, Yarmouth, Mass. (David Fried, architect for both)

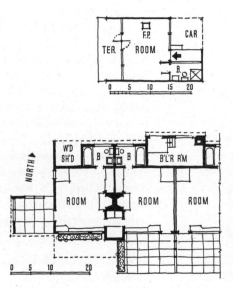

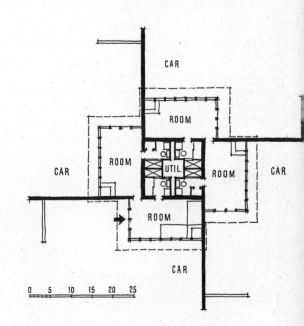

MATERIALS, FINISHES, COLORS

Floors: Asphalt tile is a favorite in newer installations. Some installations with radiant heat in floor slabs have had difficulty with indentation when temperatures overrun desirable limits. Vibrated concrete tiles about 18 in. square with integral color make a handsome, durable floor. Project floor area must be large to justify fabrication. Many recent motor courts and motor hotels use wall-to-wall carpet, often with small overall pattern to minimize accidental spotting. Wall-to-wall carpets are much easier to maintain and less hazardous than rugs. Finish floor beneath may be less expensive. Preferred installation of carpet shows narrow peripheral strip of floor and carpet is not tacked down.

Walls: Rough plaster, painted with a non-gloss washable paint, is most practical and inexpensive. Attempts to simulate paneling or board walls always look cheap and are out of scale in these necessarily small rooms.

warmer hues which would be too hot for sunny rooms.

Doors and trim in hotels and courts are often stained quite dark to avoid showing hand marks. This makes them "jump out" of a light wall and clutters up the room visually. Wood grain in itself (even if light) will reduce effect of hand marks more than paint. To avoid disappointments, room color schemes should not be established until available stock furniture and venetian blind finishes are reviewed and a selection is made.

EQUIPMENT

Furniture and furnishings: The majority of new and recently decorated courts have standard flush-metal hotel furniture of excellent quality with best grade mattresses and springs. This kind of equipment, complete, will cost approximately $600.00 per double room, including carpet. Some courts are using the dolly or Hollywood type of bed with no footboard. These have large casters to facilitate housekeeping. All furniture should have rustproof glides.

Extra bed capacity may be provided by sofa beds or

by folding utility beds (Rollaways) which jack-knife the mattress vertically and can be rolled around easily on 3-in. rubber casters. Frames take regular twin-bed size mattresses 3 ft 3 in. and are usually supplied with a less expensive grade since use is not so continuous and durability is not critical.

Many courts furnish full size dressers with several drawers which are never opened by guests who stay only one night. There is some feeling that a psychologically homelike effect is achieved in this way. A combination vanity-desk with two drawers just large enough to hold an extra pair of blankets makes much more sense. The same functions may be provided by simple built-in vanity-desk shelf and cabinet or open shelves (easily checked by maid). Some operators prefer not to leave extra blankets in rooms.

be sufficient. If there are two arm chairs add one floor lamp.

Bathrooms: All-tile bathrooms (about $400 for tile-work) are required for top grading by the better associations because of superior maintenance. Large stall-type showers with built-in wing wall obviating need for curtain are also preferred. This could be provided by carefully detailed screen of obscure corrugated glass. Points to watch: support, free edge, transition from corrugations to base. A veteran traveler commented recently on need for some method of quickly heating shower stall floors in winter-time in rental units. The dense shower floor never heats up unless a wasteful amount of hot water (if available) is run on it. This steams up the whole bathroom.

Maynard Parker

Robert Cleveland

Typical guest accommodations: left, Tucson Biltmore (Arthur T. Brown, Archt.); right, Santa Ynez Inn, Los Angeles (Alfred Gilman, Archt.)

No stock furniture finishes will withstand everything — the best available for general service will not resist acetone-type nail-polish removers. Many courts add plate-glass tops. If these are supplied locally, be sure to specify edges ground and top beveled — grinding alone leaves a sharp arris.

Two luggage racks should be provided for a double room and they should have a rear curb of some sort as well as bumpers or projecting rear legs to hold luggage and rack away from wall or foot of bed. Stock chairs are now available designed so that they will not mar walls (rear legs project beyond line of back).

Typical double room should provide: 2 double beds, 1 night table, 1 combination vanity-desk with mirror, 2 luggage racks (one can be used as vanity bench), 1 arm chair (2 better), 1 straight chair, 2 lamps, 1 waste basket, regional maps on wall.

Lighting: If wall outlets are wired to switch from doorway, ceiling light may be omitted. One lamp on night table and one on desk (shared by arm chair) will usually

Carports or garages: Ultra-violet rays of sunlight, condensation of dew, evaporation of rain, freezing and thawing of snow and ice, spotting by birds, trees and insects, and salt atmosphere are all harmful to automobile finishes. These destructive elements indicate the desirability of keeping cars in closed garages. But the motor court patron is a transient; the garage is by no means a necessity for a motor court; unless the climate is extreme, carports or open parking will be acceptable. A higher rating, however, will be granted by associations for garages.

When carports are provided at the ends of grouped rental units, the transition to the next building may require special detailing, particularly if there is variation in site grades. Doubling up supports is awkward and such central posts are subject to battering by inaccurate drivers. It is much simpler to forget about having a clean, repetitive unit building, and frankly design a bridged shelter between the two buildings.

There is no need to plaster soffits of carports unless it is felt that the additional fire resistance is essential.

MOTELS

CONSTRUCTION NOTES

Foundations: Dense concrete block on poured footings make satisfactory foundations for these predominantly one-story structures.

Walls: 8-in. cinder blocks with or without plaster and/or stucco and with or without furring, depending on climate, are used in majority of better jobs. A number of reliable block paints are available which apparently do a good job of waterproofing unplastered block. Integrally-colored concrete brick units, brick backed up with 4-in. cinder block, brick veneer and frame are also used.

insulation job often neglected is between backed-up medicine cabinets.

WEATHER CONSIDERATIONS

Orientation: Studied location and area of fenestration, provision of calculated hoods and screens for sun control, and consideration of prevailing seasonal winds can make considerable difference in heat load and summer and/or winter comfort. Architects cannot afford to be unfamiliar with latest developments in this field which has a constantly growing documentation.

Heating: An increasing use of radiant panel heating is noted, with source in floor slab. This location is not considered ideal by many heating engineers, who prefer ceiling panels. Time lag is much longer in floor (heating and cooling off) and floor finishes are sometimes not appropriate (carpet, softening materials). Many motor courts are located in natural gas areas and use individual

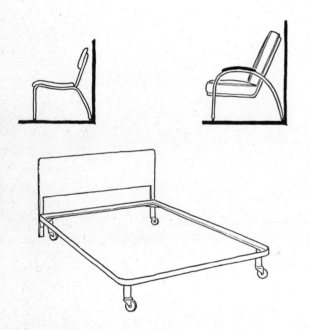

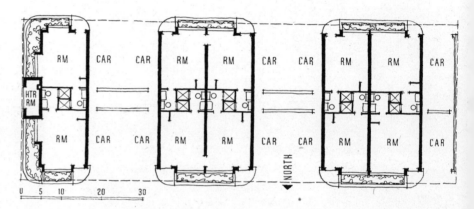

Left, satisfactory types of standard furniture: chairs with rear legs projecting to prevent marred walls, simple metal "dolly" bed. Plan above: Motel Pam, near Columbus, Ohio (Tibbals-Crumley-Musson, Archts.), essentially a double-unit scheme with variations. Utility core down center is lighted by clerestory. Split heating (part radiant, part radiators) is designed to prevent frozen plumbing in unrented units in winter

Floors: Slabs on grade with asphalt tile finish are very frequently found.

Partitions: 4- or 6-in. cinder block with or without plaster (much better sound reduction with plaster but inexpensive, attractive and easily maintained texture without).

Ceilings: Gypsum board, acoustic board or tile are common. Natural finish flush wood boards can give pleasant relief from white ceilings. Painted wood plank roofs with exposed beams (mill construction) are used in some "ranch-type" structures.

Sound Control: Planning with entries, closets and baths between rental units is common. One sound-

gas-burning units. These, when unvented, have given much trouble, ranging from excessive condensation to fatalities. Effective new vented units are available which heat room without exposed flame. Radiant baseboard heating is becoming more popular.

Ventilation: Planning for cross-ventilation or "right-angle ventilation" is usual in warmer climates and recognized in motor court publicity as a selling point which the city hotel can offer to only a few guests. Electric fans mounted on a high wall bracket are effective, and out of the way of children and pets.

Air conditioning: Southern and Southwestern courts and motor hotels are often 100 per cent air conditioned and could not hold their business without this feature.

One extensive court in a Middle Atlantic state, with forced hot-water heating pipes run underground in tile (24 in. minimum depth) from heating plant to individual cottages and to restaurant unit-heaters, discovered that, in summertime, water in the pipes was 60° and gave considerable cooling effect when circulated through the unit-heaters in dining room.

Rainfall: Driveway, parking and general site drainage is extremely important since guests enter rooms directly from outdoors and room maintenance work can be tripled by muddy shoes. There is also a psychologically bad effect in driving into a motor court on a rainy evening and finding pools of water everywhere.

Snow removal: If project is in a snow region, and is extensive, a Jeep with 5- or 6-ft-wide snowplow attachment (standard accessory available in either width) will be invaluable.

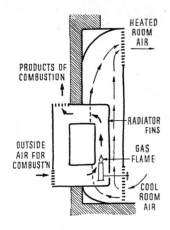

Standard type of unit heater for motels burns piped or bottled gas, must be on outside wall; combustion air is separate from room air

Joyce Studio

Joyce Studio

Above, two views of Motel Pam showing covered car parking, continuous roof. Right, cars parked at door but not under roof, George Washington Motor Court, Fredericksburg, Va. (R. R. Sollenberg, Designer). Lower right, individual carports, but units so close together that a common roof (see Motel Pam above) would seem more sensible

PROMOTIONAL FEATURES

As hotels have done before them, motor courts now compete with each other (and with hotels) by offering many special amenities and services. Some of these are quite small gadgets but are helpful and remembered by guests. Following are typical items:

Telephone or intercom with switchboard
Room radios (coin-operated type is resented by some guests)
Electric fans
Ironing board, outlet (note current)
Razor outlet
Individual small refrigerators (wall type)
Bottle opener
Shoe cleaner
Flyswatter
Touring information: maps and guides

Pawley

M O T E L S

Robert Cleveland

Gift shop
Auto service and filling station
Laundry service
Diaper service
Valet
Ice service (cube maker or bulk cube box)
Soft drink vending machine
Free cool drink on arrival, free morning coffee

Playground equipment
Badminton
Tennis
Shuffleboard
Golf (putting course)
Swimming pool

Skating
Lounge (fireplace,
    magazines, radio,
    television)
Game room
Ping pong or deck tennis

Signs and advertising: The following media should
have design study:
Highway signs; entrance sign(s); vacancy and no-
vacancy signs (note particularly problem of association
emblems); directional signs on project; regional character items.

Recreation and entertainment: In general, recreation areas should not be near enough to rental units to
disturb sleep. Since they are promotional in nature it is
good to have them visible from highway; but safety
must also be considered.

Pets: While not strictly promotional, management
policy toward pets is of definite importance to guests
traveling with animals. Some operators rent only certain
units to pet-owners (to be able to reassure subsequent
guests with allergies, etc., that *their* quarters have not
been so occupied) — some merely ask for cooperation
indoors and put up signs about the shrubbery. Others
flatly refuse to rent to pet-owners, advertise the fact
and save something on maintenance at the cost of turning away such business. Some resort hotels provide
kennels.

NOTES ON FOOD OPERATIONS

Detailed data on roadside restaurants is outside the
scope of this study but references on the subject are

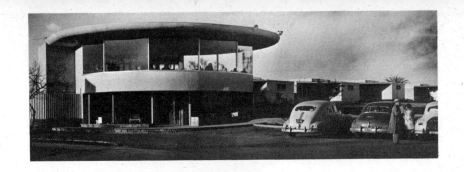

Maynard Parker

Julius Shulman

Such facilities as restaurants and service stations are not considered satisfactory adjuncts of the average motel except as promotional items. However, just to prove the rule, in quite a few cases this type of accommodation has been found exceptionally profitable. In many instances, climate, locale, custom, or a special talent has been exploited. On the facing page are shown five dining areas in Santa Ynez Inn near Los Angeles, one of them a pool-side terrace (Alfred Gilman, Archt.). The four photos above, of the Tucson Biltmore, Tucson, Ariz. (Arthur T. Brown, Archt.), show the semi-circular dining room elevated above the central mall and swimming pool, with the 4-unit cottages, much like those shown previously in plan, in the background. Photo at left, lounge, Palm Springs Biltmore, Palm Springs, Calif. (Frederick Monhoff, Archt.)

MOTELS

given in the bibliography. It is agreed by many operators that kitchenettes are not desirable. It is extremely difficult to maintain sanitary standards with transient use and the extra attraction for vermin is just one more problem. Some courts have facilities to provide travelers with breakfast; a coffee room or counter is sufficient. Location near existing dining facilities is one answer, but if project is isolated, provision of full restaurant service becomes urgent. No one wants to get back in his car after driving 300–400 miles to look for a place to eat, after finding a place to sleep. The inconvenience will be remembered.

ASSOCIATIONS

Of the many organizations whose insignia and guidebooks indicate superior motel accommodations, two are discussed here; others are listed in the bibliography.

American Automobile Association has trained field men covering all main highways in North America. Their motel reports, analyzed on standard forms, are based on five considerations: general appearance, atmosphere, equipment, maintenance, cleanliness. The A.A.A. pamphlet, *Affiliation Requirements for Motor Courts*, tells standards to be met for listing in A.A.A.'s *Accommodations Directory*.

Quality Courts United, Inc., an operators' association, sets superior standards for industry protection. It has 128 members in Eastern seaboard states, is ten years old, requires applicants to fill out detailed *Analysis of Facilities* grading sheets. These, covering planning, landscaping, construction and equipment as well as housekeeping, etc., are checked, and acceptance further depends upon favorable action by the Board of Directors.

BIBLIOGRAPHY

KEY		
b bibliography	**m**	maps
d details, diagrams	**p**	plans
f forms	**s**	sketches
g graphs, charts	**t**	tables
	v	photos

BOOKS, PAMPHLETS

1. American Hotel Assn. Public Relations Committee. *How to Sell the Motor Traveler.* A.H.A., New York, 1948. 55pps.
2. *Architectural Record. Time-Saver Standards.* F. W. Dodge Corp., New York, 1st ed., 1946.
Residential furniture pp. 98–99, 110–111
Bathrooms 133–140
Closets 141–154
Garages 155–156
Hotel bedrooms 169–173
Restaurants, bars 176–184

Julius Shulman

Pepper Tree Inn, Palm Springs, Calif.
(Stewart Williams, Archt.), is, again,
almost a resort hotel for motorists
rather than a place for a tourist's
overnight stop. Partly two-storied, its
one-story portion provides access to
guests' rooms by means of a roofed
walk, and encircles a courtyard and
swimming pool

Architectural Record, Time-Saver Standards, continued:

Service stations	232–233
Recreation areas, pools	368–386
Orientation, solar data	401–409
Driveways, walks, steps	419–430
Garden pools	431–432
Domestic hot water	539–540
Sewage disposal	553–564
Signs (illuminated)	600–603

3. Automobile Manufacturers Assn. *Automobile Facts and Figures.* A.M.A., Detroit, 1949. 80pp. (Annual on production, use, highway data.) **gt**
4. Dahl, J. O. *Restaurant Management.* Harper & Bros., New York, 4th rev. ed. 1944. 348 pp. **fpt**
5. Dana, A. W. *Kitchen Planning.* Harper & Bros., New York, 1949. 218 pp. **pv**
6. Hamilton, F. F., *Hotel Front Office Management.* Pub. by author, Miami, Fla., 2nd ed. 1947. 436 pp. (Small hotels.) **f**
7. Horwath & Horwath. *Hotel Operations in 1948.* (17th annual study.) H.&H., New York, 1949. 48 pp. **gt**
8. Horwath, E. B. & Louis Toth. *Hotel Accounting.* The Ronald Press Co., New York, rev. ed. 1948. 483 pp. **ft**
9. Love, H. B. *Establishing and Operating a Year-Round Motor Court,* [Industrial (Small Business) Series No. 50]. U. S. Dept. of Commerce, Office of Small Business, 1945. 125 pp. **fpv**
10. National Interregional Highway Committee. *Interregional Highways, 1944 Report.* (House Document No. 379 78th Cong. 2nd Sess.) Public Roads Admin., Federal Works Agency, 1944. 184 pp. (proposed highways.) **dmv**
11. National Recreation Assn. (G. D. Butler). *Recreation Areas, Their Design and Equipment.* A. S. Barnes & Co., New York, 1947. 174 pp. **bpv**
12. Public Roads Admin. *Highway Statistics 1947* (GPO Catalog No. FW 2.2: H53/7/947). Public Roads Admin., Federal Works Agency, 1947. 106 pp. **t**
13. *Waldorf-Astoria Manuals, The.* Dahl Publishing Co., Stamford, Conn., 1947. Vol. 1: Office, apartments, clerks, etc. 203 pp. **fv**
Vol. 2: Mechanical communications, Uniformed services. 126 pp. **fv**
Vol. 3: Food service. 200 pp. **fv**
Vol. 4: Housekeeping (in press).

PERIODICALS

GENERAL ARTICLES, REFERENCE ISSUES
American Magazine:
14. "Camps of Crime," by Hoover and Cooper. Feb. 40:14–15, 130–132. **s**
Architectural Record:
15. "Highway Hotels," Building Types Study No. 103. July 45:66–79. **ps**
16. "Hotels," Building Types Study No. 81. Sept. 43:67–82. **dpv**
17. "Hotels," Building Types Study No. 85. Jan. 44:52–70. (Modernization, planning, equipt.) **psv**
18. "Hotel Laundries," Time-Saver Standards. Jan. 44:93–94. **pd**
19. "Motels Move Into the Select Circle". May 48:95–117. (Examples.) **pv**
Beaux-Arts Inst. of Design Bulletin:
20. "A Motel" (B.A.I.D. Program), by H. H. Harris. Oct. 45:18–21. **ptv**
21. Criticism (B.A.I.D. Class B Program), by C. C. Braun. Oct. 45:18. (Motels.)
Fortune
22. "Hotel Design," by George Nelson. Sept. 47:106–109, 140, 143. (Hotel faults, maintenance, design.) **gmv**
23. "That Hotel Boom." Sept. 47:103–105 + overrun. (Finance, statistics.) **g**

Hotel Management
24. "Analyzing Your House For Efficiency," by E. E. Post. Dec. 47:28–32, 76, 84, 90. (Checklist of hotel planning, structure, equipment.) **p**
25. "Before You Invest — Investigate," by E. E. Post. Aug. 48:67–70. (Highway hotel projects.) **ps**
26. "Building Highway Hotels and Motor Courts That Will Pay Dividends," by H. E. Werner, Archt. Aug. 48:34–47, 94, 100 (Financial data on Santa Anita, Arcadia, Cal., pp. 48–49; 650-seat restaurant, pp. 50–53, **pv**; 44-seat drive-in, pp. 53–55, **pv**). **pv**
27. Reference Issue on Motor Courts. July 45.
28. "Why Many Downtown Hotel Guests Are Switching to Motor Courts," by Hattie and Constance Plemons. Apr. 49:49–51, 106. (Business success at Motor Inn, Wichita Falls, Tex., services provided, travelers' statements.) **v**
29. "Why More and More Tourists Are Turning to Motels," by R. P. Bryant. Aug. 47:32–36. **ps**
Motels and Courts
30. "18 Points for Motor Court Operators." Feb. 49:16–17, 22.
31. "Here's Looking at You Through the Eyes of Hotel Men," by Stuart Todd. Nov. 48:9, 22; Dec. 48:10, 12, 23; Jan. 49:9, 16.
32. "Lo! How the Mighty Have Fallen," by Stuart Todd. July 49:7, 20. (Comment on recognition of motor courts.)
33. "The Payoff," by Stuart Todd. Mar. 49:5, 24.
34. "Standards for Tourist Courts," by Mark McMillin. Aug. 48:6, 14. (United Motor Courts Assn. standards.)
Motor News (Detroit A.A.A.)
35. "Hotels and the Traveler," by Creighton Peet. Feb. 49:8–9, 23. (Services for motorists.) **v**
Nation's Business
36. "A Car Hotel and Hot Water Too," by R. M. Henry. Sept. 47:101. **v**
Reader's Digest
37. "Thrivin' Drive-Inns." Sept. 47:84–86. (Motor court industry expansion, reasons for popularity.)
Saturday Evening Post
38. "Just What the Motorist Ordered," by F. J. Taylor. July 5, 47:32–33, 90, 93. (Motor court, Bakersfield, Cal.) **v**
Tourist Court Journal
39. American Hotel Association proposal to meet tourist court competition. June 48:3, 16; Aug. 48:3; Dec. 48:5, 28.
40. A.H.A. Survey Report. Dec. 47:18–19. (Recommendations to hotels to meet motor court competition.)
41. "Generalizations On Tourist Court Requirements," by H. W. Peaslee, Archt. Nov. 45:11–12, 24. (Layout, admin.) **s**
42. "Looking Forward," by H. B. Love. Aug. 45:17. (18 suggestions for motels by Duncan Hines.)
43. "Salesmen's Questions." Mar. 48:5, 22. (Accommodation requirements of firm with national sales force.)

EXAMPLES — NEW ENGLAND
44. South Yarmouth, Mass., Cabins. David Fried, Archt. *Progressive Architecture,* Dec. 47:55–57. (6 2-br. cabins.) **pv**

EXAMPLES — SOUTH ATLANTIC
45. Return Motor Court, New Market, Va. C. W. Wenger, Archt. *Motels & Courts,* Feb. 49:5. (8 units, utility building.) **v**
46. Colony Inn, So. of Richmond, Va. *Tourist Court Journal,* May 44:5–7, 10–11. (Colonial Inn with cottages. 32 units, 12 in cottages, restaurant.) **s**

47. Mount Vernon Motor Lodge, W. Palm Beach, Fla. *Tourist Court Journal,* May 45:5–9. (44 units, E-plan.) **pv**

EXAMPLES — EAST SOUTH CENTRAL
48. Bozeman's Court and Restaurant, Nashville, Tenn. *Motels & Courts,* Oct. 48:23. (26 units.) **v**

EXAMPLES — EAST NORTH CENTRAL
49. Motel Pam, Columbus, Ohio. Tibbals-Crumley-Musson, Archts. *Tourist Court Journal,* Nov. 47:4–7, 30. (10 units, 3 buildings.) **pv**

EXAMPLES — WEST NORTH CENTRAL
50. "Easy Servicing Features Motel for Year-Round Occupancy," White Bear, Minn. N. R. Johnson, Archt. *American Builder,* Mar. 49:84–85. (Double cross plan, interior access to units.) **dpv**

EXAMPLES — WEST SOUTH CENTRAL
51. "A One-Story Hotel for a Texas Town," Dow Hotel for Dow Chemical Co., Freeport, Tex. A. B. Dow, Archt. *Architectural Record,* Jan. 44:67–68. (23 rooms.) **pv**
52. Tower Courts, Falfurrias, Tex. Ford & Rogers, Archts. *Tourist Court Journal,* Oct. 48:5–9, 20. (4 units.) **pv**

EXAMPLES — MOUNTAIN:
53. Bradley Skytel, Boise, Idaho. *Tourist Court Journal,* July 49:10–11, 25, 26, 37. (14 units, private plane parking.) **pv**
54. "Resort Hotel For Postwar Travelers." Wurdeman & Becket, Archts. *Architectural Record,* Aug. 44:74–76. (Bungalows behind resort hotel, Las Vegas, Nev.) **ps**
55. El Rey Hotel, Cedar City, Utah. *Motels & Courts,* Mar. 49:9. **v**

EXAMPLES — PACIFIC:
56. Motor Hotel, Long Beach, Cal. W. T. Dreiss, Desnr. *Progressive Architecture,* June 48:68, **v**; Nov. 48:65–67. (Two-wing plan; one housekeeping unit, 6 one-room units in each.) **pv**
57. Calistoga Motel, Napa Valley, Cal. J. H. Garrott, Archt. *Architect & Engineer,* May 47:16–17. (Rental units, tavern, dining room.) **ps**
58. Beverly-Carlton Hotel, Beverly Hills, Cal. S. Reisbord, Archt. *Architectural Forum,* Feb. 49:105–109. (3-story apartment hotel, patio, swimming pool.) **dpv**
59. El Rancho Sacramento. F. W. Green, Archt. *Architect & Engineer,* Sept. 47:25–27. (56 units, pool.) **v**
60. Tropic Palms Hotel, W. Los Angeles, Cal. B. A. Schutt, Archt. *Architectural Record,* May 48:110–113, **pv**; *Hotel Management,* Oct. 48:76–77. (44 units.) **pv**
61. Carl's Sea Air, Santa Monica, Cal. B. A. Schutt, Archt. *Architectural Record,* May 48:107–109. **pv**
62. Carmel Valley Inn, Monterey, Cal. R. R. Jones, Archt. *Architectural Record,* May 48:102–106; *Hotel Management,* Oct. 48:78–81. (24 units, restaurant, pool.) **pv**
63. Paso Robles Inn, Cal. *Hotel Management,* Jan. 46:36–39, 108. (Two-story bldgs., 6–12 units each, angled plan, restaurant, coffee shop.) **pv**
64. Casa Munras Hotel & Cottages, Monterey, Cal. *Hotel Management,* Oct. 47:40–43, 96. (160 room project, recreation facilities.) **pv**
65. Carousel House, Laguna Beach, Cal. Massen & Greene, Owner-desnrs. *Hotel Management,* Mar. 48:47–51. (Small motor court.) **pv**

66. Villa Hermosa, Palm Springs, Cal. Clark & Frey, Archts. *Architectural Record*, Feb. 48:116–119. (20 units, two-story, pool.) **pv**
67. The Westerner. Boyd Georgi, Archt. *Tourist Court Journal*, Mar. 49:6–8, 34, 37. **v**
68. Motel El Rancho, Fresno, Cal. (Hull Hotel Chain). *Tourist Court Journal*, May 46:5–7, 24. (80 units, restaurant, dining-dancing patio, pool.) **v**

EXAMPLES — FOREIGN:
69. Holiday Hotel, Tijuca, near Rio de Janeiro. Roberto Bros., Archts. *Architectural Forum*, Nov. 47:72–73 **pv**; *Progressive Architecture*, Dec. 48:56–60, **pv**; *Architectural Review*, Dec. 47:185–188.
70. Tourist Hotel, Ouro Preto, Brazil. O. Niemeyer, Archt. *Architectural Forum*, Nov. 47:71. **pv**

EXAMPLES — PROJECTS:
71. "Airport Hotel." J. G. Carr, Archt. *Architectural Record*, July 45:78–79. **dps**
72. "Motor Traveler's Hotel." Wiley, Fletcher & Fletcher, Archts. *Architectural Record*, July 45:75–77. **dps**
73. "Design for the Northeast." Robin & Vogel, Archts. *Hotel Management*, Aug. 48:66–67. (30-room highway hotel, restaurant, grille room.) **ps**
74. "How $315,000 Can Build This 50-Room Highway Hotel Today." J. B. Gander, Design Inc. *Hotel Management*, Aug. 48:61–65. **pv**
75. "Two Versions of an Outpost Inn." G. McS. Jackson, Desnr. *Hotel Management*, Aug. 48:56–60. (Standard and deluxe plans, unit room study.) **ps**

TECHNICAL ARTICLES:
Architectural Record:
76. "A (filling) Station for a Highway Hostelry." H. H. Harris, Archt. Feb. 44:78–80. (Shopping center, truck yard, drivers' dormitory, tourist cabins.) **ps**
77. "Airport Restaurants." J. G. Carr, Archt. Oct. 45:108–110. (Time-Saver Standards, pp. 122, 123, 125.) **pv**
78. "Analysis of Restaurant Space and Layout." Sumner Spaulding, Archt. Oct. 45:105–107. **ds**
79. "Critical Clearance Dimensions For Automobiles." Time-Saver Standards, Oct. 47:157. **t**
80. "Drive-in Restaurants and Luncheonettes," Building Types Study No. 117. Sept. 46:99–114. **psv**
81. "Highway Restaurants." F. R. Keally, Archt., and A. W. Dana, Kitchen conslt. Oct. 45:102–104. **ps**
82. "Insulation of Concrete Floors in Dwellings." Time-Saver Standards, Jan. 48:120, 123, 125. **dt**
83. "Poured Resilient Flooring for Houses." Jan. 48:115–116. **v**
84. "Progress In House Heating Equipment," by Clifford Strock. Apr. 49:139–145. **v**
85. "Restaurants," Building Types Study No. 139. July 48:119–142. **pv**
86. "Restaurants and Bars," Building Types Study No. 127. July 47:96–121. **pv**
87. "Second Thoughts on Radiant Heating," by Chapman and Fischer. Mar. 49:133–135, 176, 178. **dg**
88. "West Coast Innovations In Swimming Pool Design." Dec. 48:143–144. **dv**
Hotel Management
89. "Planning Roadside Inns For Today's New Patronage." Francis Keally, Archt. Oct. 45:30–32. (Restaurant; pp. 32–33, 126, Kitchen by A. W. Dana.) **ps**
Motels and Courts
90. "How to Melt Snow," by Ernest

Dench. Jan. 49:7, 14.
91. "Is a Court Restaurant Practical?" by Raymond Schuessler. Sept. 48:7, 23. **v**
92. "Kitchens, Pro and Con," by A. S. Cohoon. Aug. 48:12, 22.
93. "Motel Books & Their Keeping," by Stuart Todd. Sept. 48:14–15. **f**
94. "Promotion Methods," by Raymond Schuessler. Apr. 49:7, 19.
95. "Technique of Highway Sign Advertising," by Raymond Schuessler. Jan. 49:4.

Tourist Court Journal
96. "Advertising and Selling a Tourist Court." Apr. 45:5–9, 18–19. **s**
97. "Fill 'er Up!" Feb. 45:9–11. (Service Stations for tourist courts.) **s**
98. "Landscaping & Beautifying." Mar. 45:5–13, 18–19, 22. **p**
99. "Let's Eat." Dec. 44:9–12. (Coffee room operation.) **s**
100. "Lighting the Modern Motel," by W. D. Riddle. Nov. 44:5–7. **s**
101. "Linen," by G. H. Stevenson. July 38:5–7. (Bedding.) **v**
102. "Location of the Future." July 44:5–9, 14. (Motel location factors.) **ms**
103. "Planning a Tourist Court," by T. E. Lightfoot, Archt. Aug. 44:5–11, 19. **pv**
104. "Plant & Prune," by L. R. Kuykendall. Mar. 46:4–6, 29. (Landscaping.) **sv**
105. "Postwar Furnishings," by Earl Crawford. Jan. 45:5–7, 13. De Anza Motor Inn, Santa Barbara, Cal. Cliff May, desnr. **sv**
106. "Make It Hot; Then Cool." Sept. 44:5–10. (Plumbing, heating, cooling.) **d**
107. Name Preferences. Sept. 48:12. (Questionnaire results.)
108. "So You Want to Finance a Court." June 44:5–7, 11.
109. "Tourist Court Plumbing." Oct. 44:5–8, 18. **pv**

STATISTICS
American Magazine
110. 1948 Travelogue. The Crowell-Collier Publishing Co. 250 Park Avenue, New York 17, N. Y. (Travel preferences, plans.)
Automotive Industries
111. "Total Passenger Car Registrations 1935–1948." Mar. 15, 49:91. **t**
Hotel Management
112. "Hotel Dollar, The," by Horwath and Horwath. Jan. 49:44. (Charts averaging operation expenses and sales.) **g**
113. "Vacation Preferences." Jan. 47:27–30. (Data from *Holiday Magazine* survey, 1946.) **v**
114. "What Lies Ahead For 1949 In Hotel Sales and Profits," by P. B. B. Andrews. Jan. 49:33–35, 112, 114. **gt**
Motels & Courts
115. "American Travel Methods" (Abstract of No. 111). Apr. 49:2.
116. "Florida Motor Court Statistics." Oct. 48:15.
Public Roads
117. "National System Of Interstate Highways." Sept. 47:19–20. (Map 14x20. GPO Catalog No. FW 2.12:H53/8.) **m**
118. "Summer Traffic Survey, 1947." Mar. 49:148–149. **g**
119. "Trends In Motor Vehicle Travel 1936–1945," by G. P. St. Clair. Oct.-Nov.-Dec. 46:261. Same 1946: Mar. 48:45, 49, 52. Same 1947: Mar. 49:156–160. **g**
Survey of Current Business
120. "Airline Passenger Miles." 1947 Supplement: 104 (1935–1946) **t**; Dec. 47:S-22 (1947) **t**; June 49:S-22 (1948). **t**
121. "Foreign Travel Statistics." 1947 Supplement: (1935–1946) monthly averages. **t**; Dec. 47:S-23 (1947) **t**; June 49:S-23 (1948). **t**
122. "Hotel Operating Statistics." May 48:S-23 (1947) **t**; June 49:S-23 (1948). **t**

123. "Income Survey By States and Regions 1929–47." Sept. 48:10–21. **t**
124. "National Parks Visitors Statistics." 1947 Supplement: (1935–1946) monthly averages. **t**; May & Sept. 48:S-23 (1947) **t**; June 49:S-23 (1948). **t**
125. "Passenger Car Registrations." Apr. 49:3.
126. "Railroad Passenger Miles." 1947 Supplement: 107 (1935–1946) **t**; Dec. 47:S-22 (1947) **t**; June 49:S-23 (1948). **t**
127. "Railroads In The Postwar Economy." May 48:16–21. (Passenger mile data.) **g**
Tourist Court Journal
128. "Annual Operating Averages For Tourist Courts." July 49:6–9. 26; July 48:5; Aug. 46:4–7; July 45:5–6, 19; Sept. 44:13; July 43:10. **g**
129. "Let's Not Spread 'Em Too Awful Thin." July 49:28–29. (Survey statistics, San Diego area.)
U. S. News & World Report
130. "Better Vacations This Year." May 6, 49:22–23. (Travel statistics.)

SOURCES

ASSOCIATIONS, PUBLISHERS OF LISTS:
131. *American Automobile Assn.*, Pennsylvania Ave. & 17th St. NW, Washington, D. C. Annual, *Accommodations Directory*.
132. *American Hotel Assn.*, 221 W. 57th St., New York 19, N. Y.
133. *American Motel Assn., Inc.*, 1060 Broad St., Newark 2, N. J. Motel guide.
134. *American Motor Hotel Assn.*, 306 New Moore Bldg., San Antonio 5, Tex. *Travelog*, highway atlas.
135. *Duncan Hines, Inc.*, Box 548, Bowling Green, Ky. Guidebook, *Lodging for a Night*.
136. *New England Council*, Statler Bldg., Boston, Mass. *Road map guide book of New England, New York & Quebec*.
137. *Northeastern Cabin Owners Assn., Inc.*, 83 Highland St., Plymouth, N. H. Leaflet map, list (gives 294 members).
138. *Quality Courts United, Inc.*, McKays Hotel Court, Ocala, Fla. (128 courts).
139. *United Motor Courts*, 1460 Pennsylvania, Denver 3, Col. Motor travel guide.
140. Walker, R. A., Pub., Haverhill 1, Mass. *Recommendations*, annual. (1948–49 has 294 listings in Eastern U. S., Canada.)

HOTEL ACCOUNTANTS:
141. Harris, Kerr, Forster & Co., 18 E. 48th St., New York 17, N. Y.
142. Horwath & Horwath, 41 E. 42nd St., New York 17, N. Y.

MAPS:
143. *Public Roads Admin.*, Federal Works Agency, Supt. of Documents GPO, Washington, D. C. Transportation, traffic flow maps. *Roads, Price list No. 45*.
144. Oil Companies' Touring Services: Free maps, guides and information. *Conoco Travel Bureau*, Denver, Col. *Esso Touring Service*, 15 W. 51st St., New York 19, N. Y. *Shell Touring Service*, 50 W. 50th St., New York 20, N. Y.

In addition to periodicals listed before, the reader is referred to *American Motel Magazine*, new publication of the Patterson Publishing Co., 5 S. Wabash St., Chicago, Ill.; and to *Traffic Volume Trends*, monthly statistical leaflet of the Public Roads Admin., Supt. of Documents, GPO, Washington, D. C.

For Indices to current periodicals, see: *Reader's Guide to Periodical Literature*; *Art Index*; *Industrial Arts Index*. H. W. Wilson Co., 950 University Ave., New York, N. Y.

TOURINNS, INC.

A CHAIN OF MOTOR COURTS

Malcolm G. Duncan, Architect

Joseph W. Molitor

TOURINNS, Inc., is a management firm engaged in developing and operating a nationwide system of motor courts, with the intent of providing the quality of accommodations and services found in the metropolitan hotel while retaining the facility and accessibility of the motel. Each unit derives the benefits available from a large-scale operation, which would be beyond the scope of a purely local development. This plan is the result of approximately two years' intensive and extensive study of motorists' needs and the motel field, including analyses of motor courts, hotels, and public accommodations in general. There are now four Tourinns: at Fort Wayne, Indiana; Allentown, Pa.; Pittsburgh, Pa.; and Wilmington, Del. Of these, the first two have been in operation since last year; the others have just been completed.

Incorporated early in 1949, the organization has a long-term financing arrangement with State Mutual Life Insurance Co. of Worcester, Mass., and provides for local financial participation as well. At each Tourinns site there are a restaurant and service station — both under lease to national companies — and a group of single rooms in addition to double cottages arranged in a series of culs-de-sac much like a contemporary housing development. The site arrangement was intentional, to produce as pleasantly domestic an atmosphere as possible. The restaurant is intended to attract highway and local customers and to serve motel guests.

After the initial surveys and analyses, standards for site selection and for design and operation of the individual units were developed. Some 90 sites have been tentatively identified, usually on major highways near large population centers, about a day's driving distance apart. Quantity and nature of auto traffic, characteristics of the highway, surroundings, topography and stopping convenience were factors in site selection, as were: frontage in relation to total usable plot, existing competition, utilities, and proximity to recreation, to points of interest, to airports and other means of transportation.

The standard unit costs, at present prices, about $400,000 to build; rates are $8.00 double and $3.75 single. The double cottages can be converted to 2-room apartments in emergencies.

TOURINNS

The Tourinns unit at Allentown, Pa., is shown in these pages. Across page is a typical cul-de-sac; right, office approach; center below, air view showing site layout; bottom, typical double room in one of the cottages. Knoll Associates, Inc. designed the interiors and provided furniture, drapes, color schemes, etc. Each room has a long luggage rack rather than a chest; there are no drawers or closet doors, so guests will have little reason to leave things behind

Joseph W. Molitor

Weitner Aerophoto Service

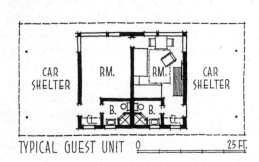

TYPICAL GUEST UNIT   0 |———————| 25 FT.

TOURINNS

On the main building's second floor are single rooms planned for such
clientele as male commercial travelers. First floor is laid out so casual
restaurant patrons need not interfere with overnight guests. In localities
where laws forbid cocktail lounges, this space becomes a private dining
room. In linen room is a launderette for guests' use

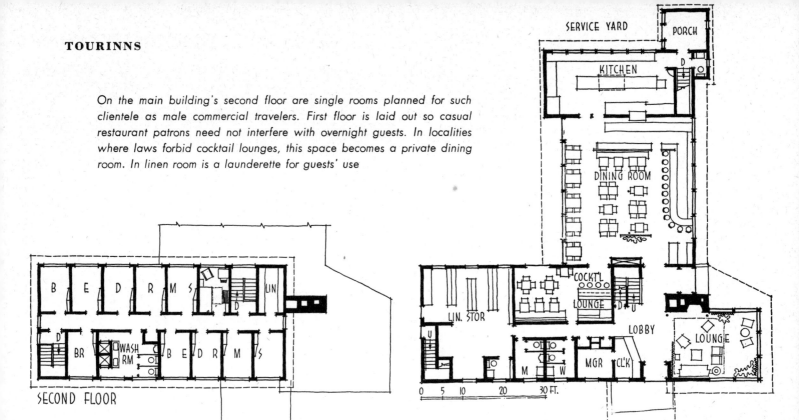

SECOND FLOOR

Joseph W. Molitor

W. Lee Moore

Landscape Architect

Right, lunch counter; below, lounge. This and the restaurant have ample glass areas, being public rooms where the quality, simplicity, and cheerful domesticity of the establishment can be displayed to potential guests. In contrast, the guest cottages are planned for privacy, set far back from traffic noises with high, small windows on exposed sides and larger windows opening to lawns and planting which, when fully developed, will screen them protectively. Even the road lights inside the area are only a few inches above ground, to avoid glare in guest rooms

Everything about a Tourinns unit is consistent in design, although in the case of the service station (right, in background) this entailed considerable work with the concessionaire. Sign, in foreground, is used repeatedly as a trademark; as it has become necessary to add items the advisability of restudying its use has become evident

For its 200th consecutive Building Types Study, ARCHITECTURAL RECORD has collaborated with the editors of *Hotel Management* magazine to provide a client's-eye view of the changing conditions encountered in the motel field by owners and operators throughout the country.

HIGHWAY HOTELS

1. **Richard's Drive-In Restaurant,**
   Boston, Mass.

2. **O'Boyle's Drive-In Restaurant,**
   Bucks Co., Pa.

3. **Red Horse Motor Inn,**
   Dayton, Ohio

4. **Motel for Max Alpert,**
   Richmond, Va.

5. **Casa Mañana Motel,**
   San Antonio, Tex.

6. **Springer Motel,**
   New Orleans, La.

7. **El Patio Motel,**
   Denver, Colo.

8. **The Shalimar Motel,**
   Miami, Fla.

9. **Juno Ranch Motel,**
   Juno Beach, Fla.

10. **Caribe Motel,**
    Miami Beach, Fla.

11. **Terrace Motor Motel,**
    Austin, Tex.

12. **Motel for Charles C. Wilmore,**
    Denver, Colo.

13. **Jack Tar Motel,**
    Galveston, Tex.

14. **Town House Motor Motel.**
    New Orleans, La.

THE NAME "GOLD COAST" has been applied to many locales, and for as many social and economic reasons through the years. The current version in Miami Beach, however, is a fashionable strip of land bristling with motels. The progeny of the stripped-down cabins of the depression years have acquired an elaborate respectability and moved up into the ranks of Big Business — in volume, capital investment and net profits. Florida's motel-building boom, for example, is reportedly spurred on by new licenses issued at the rate of three a day, and with no signs of tapering off. Indications are that a similar, though more moderate, boom is taking place in many other parts of the country. United Motor Courts, an industry association, has stated that twenty motor courts a day are being completed this year as compared with eleven a day in 1952. Today there are some 50,000 highway hotels representing a six billion dollar investment. All this activity has probably been brought about by reports of the phenomenal success of some of the older motels, and the attraction of a constantly widening range of clientele. The capture of a good percentage of the business and commercial traveler trade has been a tremendous boost to offset the traditional off-season slack periods. It was estimated that more than 86 per cent of all travelers in the U. S. went by car in 1952, and this year, some guessers predict that about 40,000,000 people, two-thirds of all those traveling by car, will stop at motels.

A pertinent point in the midst of these facts and speculations is the marked change in character of most of the new motels — both in design and operation — which should create a bumper business for architects in the field. Competition and public demand have forced motel owners to become more conscious of the high sales value of good clean design and planned efficiency. Services and extra features have been increased in some instances to the point that there is little to distinguish a motel from a hotel except its horizontal structure and the identifying sign. There is at least one case where a good sized suburban hotel, regarded as one of the white elephants left over from the late nineteen-twenties, has been refurbished a bit, equipped with a big motel sign, and currently enjoys a thriving tourist business. A number of hotel operators, conscious of the trend, have flanked their establishments with motel units which get hotel service.

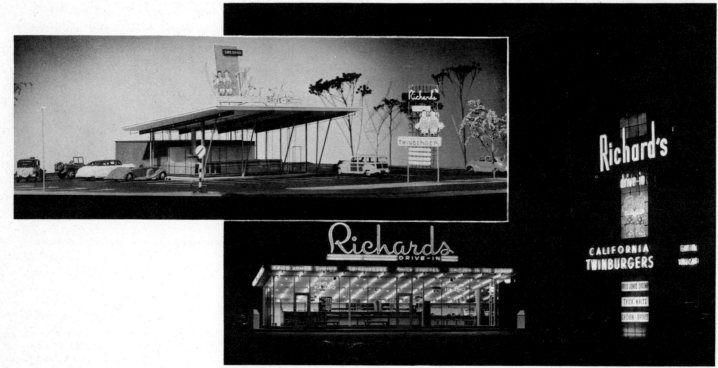

George M. Cushing, Jr.

A drive-in type of restaurant is favored by some motel operators to increase revenue. This particular example is a prototype design for Richard's Drive-In Restaurant chain by William Riseman Associates, Architects. The basic model (inset photo) will be adapted for 18 units in the Midwest and East. The photo is of one in Boston, Mass.

THE PLANNING ASPECTS of this changing concept for a motel will require the services of many more specialized professions than was the case a short while ago, when most motor courts were planned and operated by a husband-and-wife team of manager-owners. The extensive planning data for motels published in the March 1950 issue (see pages 24 through 47) are generally still quite valid as desirable factors. However, the success of many motels in apparently unfavorable locations has led to a review of a number of the points.

CONSIDERATIONS ON SITE PLANNING AND SELECTION

In the past, and in general still, it has been considered fairly disastrous to build a motel on the wrong side of a highway, with less than 500 ft frontage, on hilly sites which require expensive grading, or in a location near a number of other motor courts. Yet motels have been built and have thrived in each of these situations. The answers seem to depend on a number of factors, some local, some national. A crisply attractive, fairly priced motel, on the wrong side of a highway for the heaviest traffic, can exert a very strong pull in a shabby area of less desirable motor courts. Motels catering largely to commercial travelers can sometimes gain profit from a fairly restricted site easily accessible to the business district; and in a popular resort area, a 200-ft strip of beach can be a bonanza. Or, as a new approach, one large industrial corporation has recently built, and operates, a pleasant motel near one of its small town factories for visiting business contacts.

The increasing cooperation between better motels, and the activities of

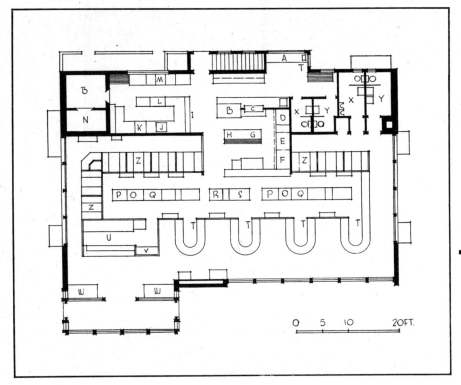

A self-service drive-in feature which eliminates car hops is an idea planned for this restaurant which might be adapted to motels. Besides regular counter and booth service, a service window is at the rear (letter A on plan) for motorists who want to eat in their cars. The restaurant, now nearing completion, was designed by Joseph J. Morgan and A. J. Varnas, Architects

LEGEND

A. "Self-Service" Pass through	I. Soiled Dishes	R. Coffee Urns
B. Ref.	J. Prewash Sink	S. Desserts
C. Pass through	K. Dishwasher	T. Water
D. Range	L. Glass Washer	U. Ice Cream
E. Fryers	M. Veg. & Pot Sinks	V. Cashier
F. Griddle	N. Freeze	W. Display
G. Sink	O. Mixer	X. Men's Toilet
H. Steam Table	P. Orange Drink	Y. Women's Toilet
	Q. Milk	Z. Booths

national motel groups have, no doubt, been responsible for the success of many improbable sites. National publicity, recommended lists, and ratings by the American Automobile Association are fostering the custom of contacting specific motels in advance for reservations, instead of the old stop-where-you-can-when-you're-tired attitude. Several national motel chains have also been established which offer more or less standardized accommodations and services, and strive to keep patrons within their own or affiliated orbits. The influence of air travel is also having its effect in some localities; resort vacationists and businessmen arrive by air, rent a car and drive to a motel where they have reserved rooms. All these items will probably gain in significance, and should be as carefully considered in choosing a site that is both economical and productive, as the now prevalent and prudent customs of checking traffic density, ease of accessibility, drainage conditions, etc.

RESTAURANTS, CONCESSIONS AND RECREATION FACILITIES

The previously held opinion that restaurants were not paying propositions in connection with motels is being reversed by many operators. The appreciation expressed by patrons who can obtain at least a quick breakfast before a day's journey has even led some motels to offer a continental breakfast free of charge. The exact type of facilities provided must still depend on local conditions, but the following arrangements have been noted: a small serving pantry for serving a light breakfast in the lobby, or in the guest rooms; more extensive use of vending machines; a small snack bar or restaurant kept open only through the lunch hour; drive-in service; and

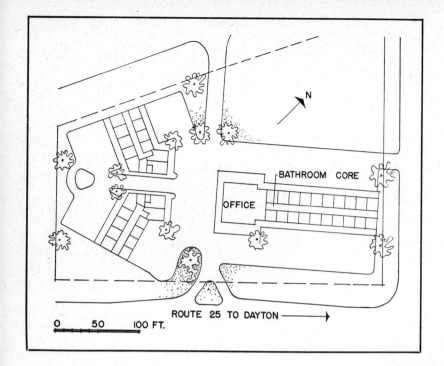

BATHROOM CORE

OFFICE

ROUTE 25 TO DAYTON →

0   50   100 FT.

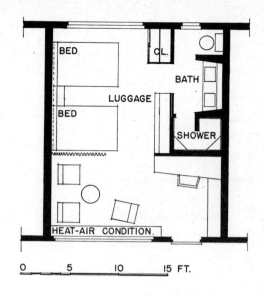

BED

CL.

BATH

LUGGAGE

BED

SHOWER

HEAT-AIR CONDITION.

0   5   10   15 FT.

Interior layouts have been carefully studied in this project for the Red Horse Motor Inn, by Joseph J. Roberto, Architect, and Caroline Kane, Interior Designer. The plan and sketch at right show the basic low-cost room unit, with casework designed for the job. TV units would be supplied on rental basis. The designers' plan for a luxury unit is at upper right

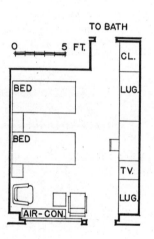

TO BATH

0   5 FT.

CL.

LUG.

BED

BED

TV.

LUG.

AIR-CON.

full-scale restaurants. The last two types, sometimes leased as a concession, might be an added source of revenue in off-seasons when there is sufficient patronage from the adjoining community. The seasonal aspects of the business, especially in resort areas, has led some owners to include facilities for small conventions, club meetings, and display rooms for salesmen to help boost year-round activity. These are matched with such hotel services as laundry and cleaning, either on the premises or by contract with a commercial laundry, private phones and switchboard service, television and radio, bars and package liquor stores, free ice cubes, and in a few cases even room service. The extent of recreational facilities provided seems to depend largely on that offered by close competition. Filling stations are still not considered desirable unless the motel is in an isolated location.

GENERAL PLANNING AND EQUIPMENT

Flexibility in the arrangement of rooms and suites has become more important with the growing variety of patronage. Commercial and resort visitors tend to prefer rooms with convertible sofa beds that serve as living rooms by day, while transient tourists prefer the standard bedroom arrange-

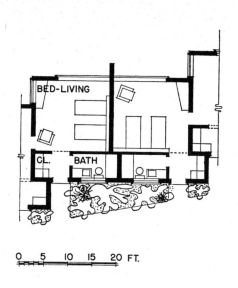

BED-LIVING

CL. BATH

0 5 10 15 20 FT.

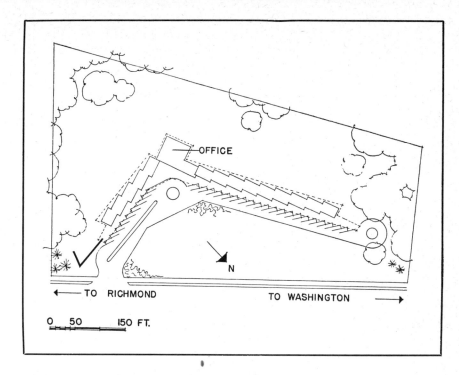

OFFICE

N

← TO RICHMOND   TO WASHINGTON →

0 50 150 FT.

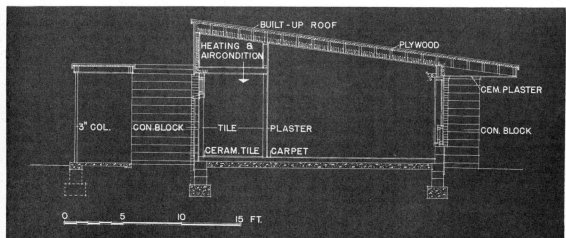

BUILT-UP ROOF

HEATING & AIRCONDITION

PLYWOOD

CEM. PLASTER

3" COL. CON. BLOCK   TILE   PLASTER

CON. BLOCK

CERAM. TILE CARPET

0 5 10 15 FT.

Privacy for room occupants has been stressed in this project by Caleb Hornbostel, Architect. Noise and lights of a car driving up and being unpacked are baffled by placing entry, closets and baths on side adjoining parking space. Adequate insulation blocks noise between units. Planned only for one-night stops, office area includes all-purpose lounge, breakfast bar

ment. Families with children often shop for motels with kitchenette facilities and have caused some owners to overlook the previous objections to increased upkeep. More and more motels are approaching hotel standards in interior furnishings, with carpeting, many lamps, fine mattresses and tile baths. Unit air conditioning and heating equipment in each room has become fairly standard in many regions as it permits easy cut-off of unrented sections. Provision of noise control, adequate privacy, and protection from the glare of headlights and electric signs are vital. However, fewer motels provide garages or carports, especially in the warmer climates.

In the midst of the rosy glow surrounding the motel business, at least one word of warning has been sounded, and a point of view that might incidentally help architects to rule out some of the more chi-chi ideas forced on them. In an article for *Hotel Management* magazine, C. Vernon Kane, partner of Horwath & Horwath, accountants, points out the present attitude of insurance and mortgage companies, who have become very cautious with regard to motels: "The more luxurious motor court may be handicapped by its better appearance. The economy-minded traveler of the future may drive into a plainer motor court in the hope of getting lower rates."

4 MOTEL FOR MAX ALPERT, RICHMOND, VA.

The motel utilizes water pumped from a deep well on the property, has its own sewage disposal system. Water system is oversized to augment fire extinguishing equipment

5 CASA MAÑANA MOTEL, SAN ANTONIO, TEX.

Each unit (typical plans at right) has individual window A.C. unit, thermostatically controlled gas wall heater. Office (above right) has PBX board, 5-ton A.C. unit

GARAGE

WORK RM.

B.R.
ST.
B.
KIT

LIVING

OFF

HTR LOGS

LOUNGE

0 5 10 15 FT.

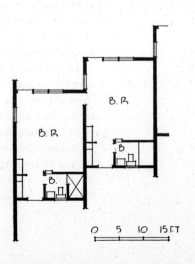

B.R.

B.R.

B.

B.

0 5 10 15 FT

STAGE ONE

Thomas B. Thompson, Architect

CASA MAÑANA MOTEL is perhaps adroitly named, for these six crisp new buildings form the nucleus for a larger motel slated to include an impressive variety of recreational and sales facilities. Adjoining properties, which also belong to the owners, will be developed with a cafe-lounge, a drive-in, a liquor store and a service station. It is also proposed to provide a swimming pool, a small golf course, picnic grounds and similar facilities along a small creek on the property. The present rental units are placed on high ground with an open vista across a valley. Each building has eight units, angled for greater privacy. End division walls between units are lightweight concrete block and serve as acoustical insulation; staggered baths are also planned to reduce noise transmission. Other walls have redwood siding. Future plans include 24 more units and development of terraces and sitting areas outside all rooms. Furnishings, color schemes and site planning are all being done by the architects.

Ulric Meisel

Each 8-unit building has central water heater. All units have showers, eight have tubs. Foundations are "floating" reinforced concrete slabs with 8- by 16-in. perimeter beams

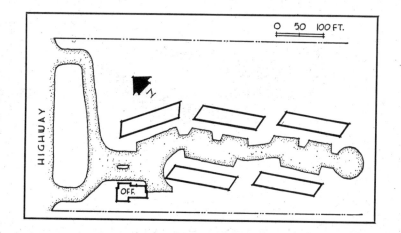

Casa Mañana interiors are also kept crisp and simple. Concrete end walls are waterproofed and painted. Other walls and doors are natural-finish gum plywood. Ceilings are painted wallboard, insulated with glass wool blankets. Floors are colored cement tile. All baths have ceramic tile floors and wainscots

REVISED PROJECT: HIGHER DENSITY FOR HIGHER RETURNS

Ricciuti, Stoffle & Associates, Architects

THE ROLE OF FINANCES in the designing of motels is plainly indicated in the development of this project to be built near New Orleans. The site, a plot 360 ft wide by 440 ft deep, had several drawbacks: it was on the wrong side of the highway for incoming traffic to the city, and was in an area with a high density of sub-standard motels. The original scheme was planned to create enough appeal to offset these factors by an informal arrangement of basic 4-unit cottages. Each unit was given a high degree of privacy by the use of small patios; elimination of windows in the front also shielded units from auto headlights. The need to provide more units eventually forced the adoption of more conventional row-type units, eliminating garages and combining recreation and office areas into one building.

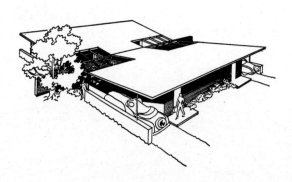

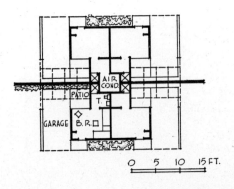

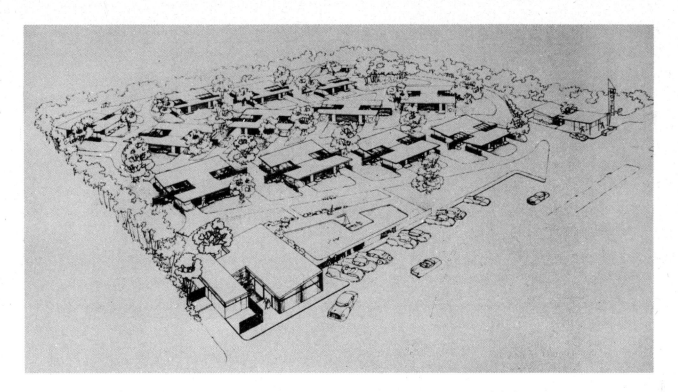

The original motel scheme (above) includes 50 units in 4-unit cottages (bottom opposite page), and separate restaurant-recreation and office-administration buildings. The revised scheme (right and below) increases capacity to 128 units, eliminates garages and patios. An effort was made to preserve an appearance of openness from the highway by using a triangular shaped lawn to give incoming traffic a full view of the combined administration-recreation building and the pool. Exterior finishes will be brick and redwood or cypress

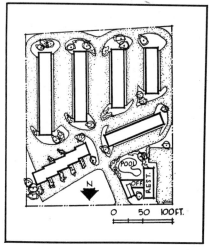

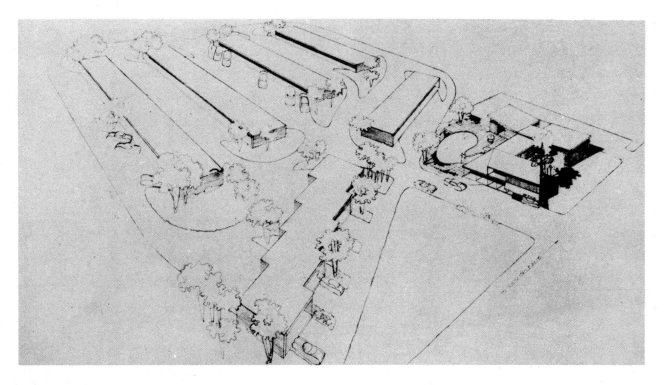

Marshall Brooks

SECOND STORY ENLARGES COMPACT MOTEL SCHEME

Charles Sink, Architect

EXTRA rental units were added and parking space preserved on the restricted site of this motel by the use of a two-story wing at the back. Sheltered access to rooms from all parts of the parking lot is provided by cloister-like covered walkways, open galleries and three stairways. A service room is at juncture of the wings.

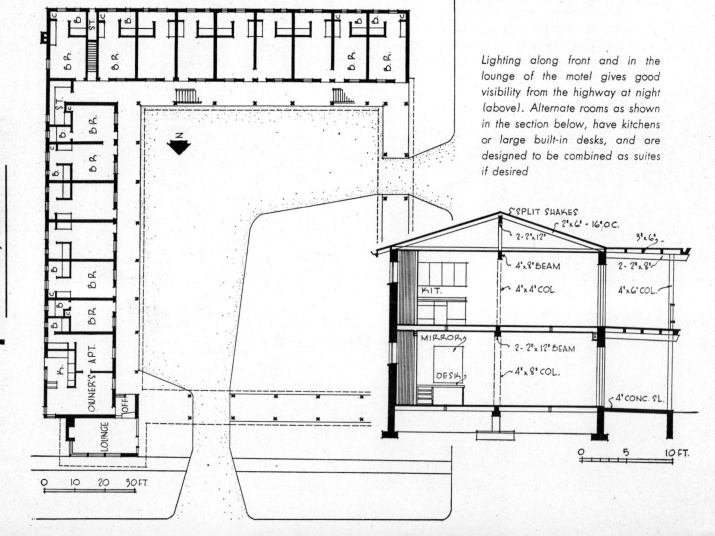

Lighting along front and in the lounge of the motel gives good visibility from the highway at night (above). Alternate rooms as shown in the section below, have kitchens or large built-in desks, and are designed to be combined as suites if desired

7 EL PATIO MOTEL, DENVER, COLO.

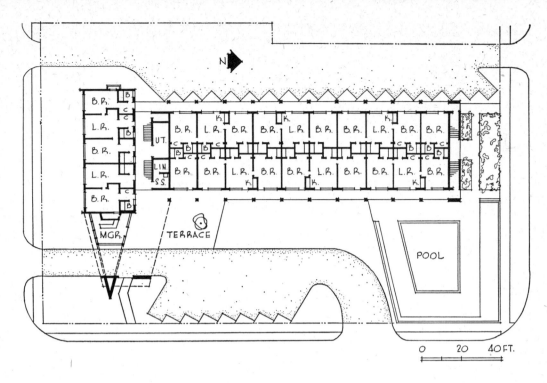

50-ROOM MOTEL PLANNED FOR LONGER STOPS

The Edwin T. Reeder Associates, Architects

THE wide range of types of tourists that can be expected in the Miami area have been taken into account in the planning of this two-story motel. Rooms are arranged so that they may be combined into apartments of one, two or three rooms to accommodate overnight guests, commercial travelers or families on a holiday. All rooms flank a bathroom core running the length of the building, and open on either the front or the rear parking lot. The second floor is identical to the first. Stairs are placed behind fins at the north end, and adjoining the service rooms. The original scheme for the front terrace and pool shown on the plan above have not yet been carried out.

8

THE SHALIMAR MOTEL, MIAMI, FLA.

Ernest Graham

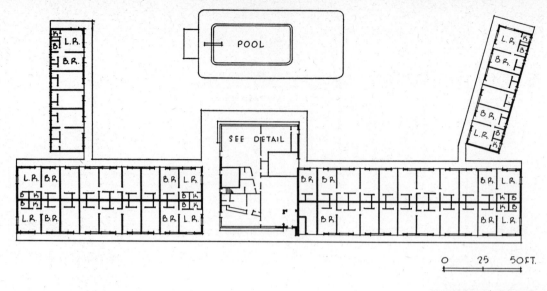

SEE DETAIL

POOL

0   25   50FT.

THE resort trade is being cultivated by motels in many areas by the added inducements of such luxuries as running ice water in the rooms, large lobbies, cocktail lounges, coffee shops, television, swimming pools and an enormous variety of recreation facilities. This one-story scheme for the Juno Ranch Motel also features double louvered windows — redwood slats outside, glass inside — individual A.C. units, covered walks around building.

TWO OCEAN FRONT RESORT MOTELS

THE Gold Coast motel strip of Miami Beach has had a phenomenal growth in the past three years. The Caribe Motel (below and right) is typically planned for a holiday atmosphere, and caters to guests who often stay for a three month vacation period. The narrow, deep site was developed with an H plan; parking area faces road in front.

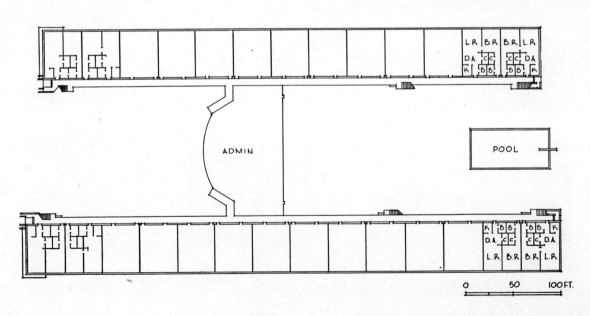

ADMIN

POOL

0   50   100FT.

The one-story Juno Ranch Motel has tall clerestory over public areas (plan below). Structure is stuccoed concrete block. Kitchen and coffee shop have access to beach

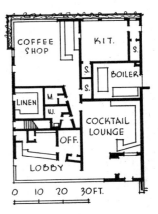

Norman M. Giller, Architect

FOR THE FLORIDA COAST

Klara Farkas

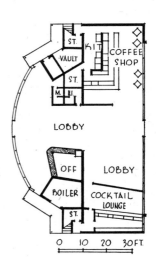

The Caribe Motel has elaborate lounges (plan above, photo above left). Wings are one room deep, have balconies on one side facing pool (photo left)

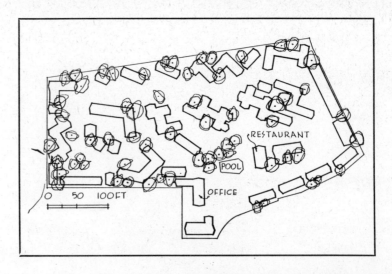

LANDSCAPING AND VARIETY KEYNOTE TEXAS MOTEL

GREAT ADVANTAGE was made of the rolling, wooded character of the site to produce this extremely pleasant, well landscaped and informal motel. The 102 units, no two of which are alike, are arranged in various sized groups made up of the basic unit plan shown on the opposite page. The units are fairly large, with separate dressing room and bath combinations and individual carports. Exteriors include combinations of the following materials: white and pink stone, red brick, vertical boards, rough or smooth boards and bats, horizontal siding, colored wood shakes and corrugated transite. Roofs are built-up with crushed red brick topping. Each building is insulated, and heated or cooled by individual units.

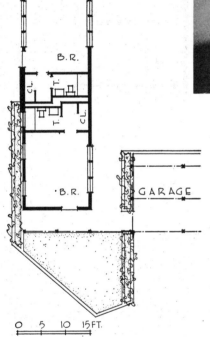

B.R.

CL. T.

T. CL.

B.R. GARAGE

0 5 10 15 FT.

All interiors were also designed by the architects. Wall surfaces include combinations of plaster and vertical boards, plywood, hand-blocked wallpapers, and wainscot. Floors are carpeted

Niggli & Gustafson,
Architects

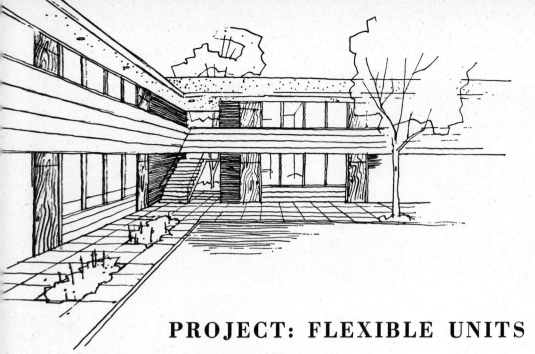

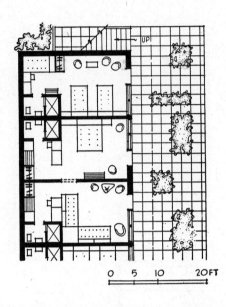

PROJECT: FLEXIBLE UNITS

Norton Polivnick, Architect

The increasing trend to automobile travel for business or pleasure trips and family vacations poses a relatively new problem for motel designers and operators to meet the varying demands for types of room arrangements. The architect of this motel project has devised an economical solution by providing a basic unit that lends itself to a variety of furniture layouts. The units have been combined into a well organized design that also includes a restaurant, a group of shops and recreation facilities. An existing service station occupies a corner of the site adjoining the restaurant.

MOTEL FOR CHARLES C. WILMORE, DENVER, COLO.

12

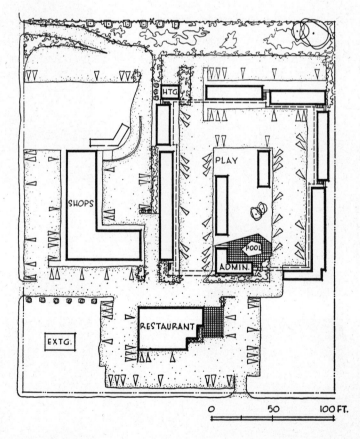

The two sketches shown here illustrate the adaptability of the basic unit to different arrangements: a sitting room with sofa beds (below), a unit with double bed (above)

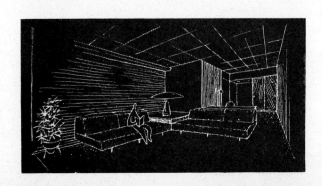

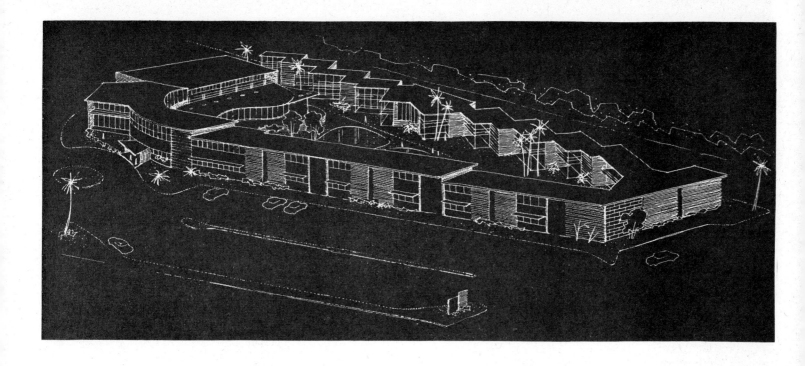

EXPANSION TO BOOST YEAR-ROUND OCCUPANCY

Thomas M. Price, Architect

The relatively short duration of the popular vacation season in many areas — in Galveston it is from May to September — can leave a resort operation with a lengthy and unprofitable slack season. Although the original portion of the Jack Tar Hotel, built in 1940 (shaded area on plan below), has had an overall success, the owners have sought a way to keep occupancy high during the off-season. The result is an addition (sketch above) designed to attract small conventions, sales meetings and club activities. The original property has 100 units; the addition has 60 suites, and expansion of restaurant and meeting room facilities.

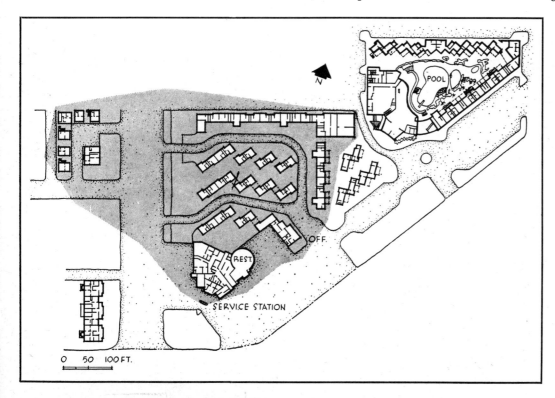

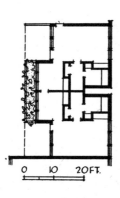

APARTMENT HOTEL COUNTERPART

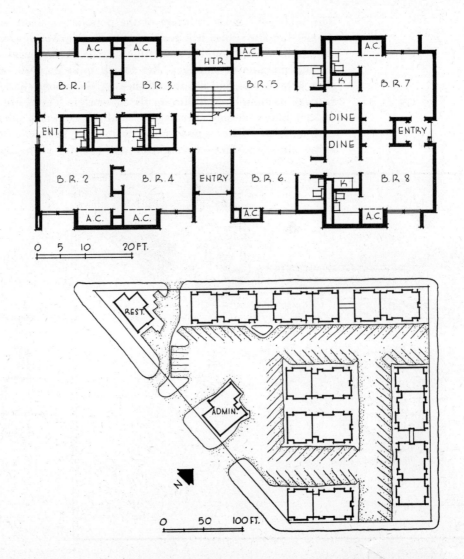

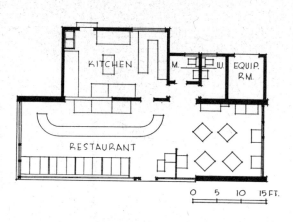

KITCHEN M. W. EQUIP. RM.

RESTAURANT

0 5 10 15 FT.

FOR MOTORISTS

Curtis and Davis,
Architects

An unusually adaptable arrangement of rooms has been worked out for this New Orleans motel to permit rental as apartments of one to four or more rooms. The rental units are grouped into eight identical buildings, which feature such items as second floor sun decks, a ¾-ton unit air conditioner in each room, and central forced circulation hot water heating. All the buildings in the project are constructed on concrete slabs on gravel fill, with wood frames, and exteriors finished with brick veneer and cedar shingles. Interiors are finished with plywood and plaster walls and plaster ceilings. Floors are asphalt tile or carpeted. All baths have ceramic tile floors and wainscots, and are equipped with bathtubs and showers.

The restaurant (above) has been located in a corner of the site adjoining a street intersection, where it will attract regular drive-in trade, as well as draw from the motel guests. A small serving pantry has also been included in the administration building (below).

Frank Lotz Miller

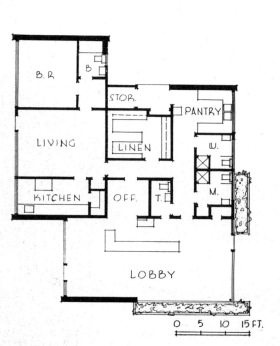

B.R. B
STOR. PANTRY
LIVING LINEN W.
KITCHEN OFF. T. M.
LOBBY

0 5 10 15 FT.

BISONTI LODGE

RESORT MOTEL

Donald J. Higgins

PALM SPRINGS, CALIFORNIA

Harry J. Williams & Assoc.; E. Stewart Williams — H. Roger Williams, Architects

In general, Palm Springs winter visitors are of two kinds: weekenders from Los Angeles (who want a comfortable minimum living-bedroom with bath) and vacationers from more distant points (couples or families needing more space; these usually ask for detached bungalows). Hence Bisonti Lodge was designed as a row of single room units plus a group of bungalows, all organized around a small patio and pool.

The best view lies to the west and southwest; the warm afternoon sun also comes from that quarter. To make the most of the view, the individual units were angled so their glazed walls would look in this direction, and they were connected by a louvered overhang to minimize sun heat. Only the single units have been built to date. As soon as regulations permit, the independent bungalows are to be constructed. The present buildings are of wood frame, with plastered walls and ceilings and carpeted concrete floors. The louvered roof overhang is of redwood. All units are electrically heated and cooled.

The project, which to date has cost just over $38,500 (or $9.04 per sq ft), has been very successful. It is usually filled to capacity during the entire season.

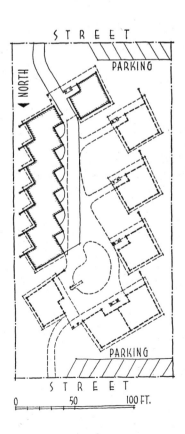

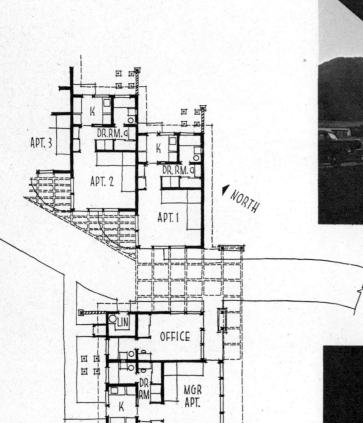

All seven of the single-room units are identical. Wood, including fir doors and frames, is painted; roof is built-up, with white surface to reflect sun. Insulation is aluminum foil and all sheet metal is aluminum

Donald J. Higgins

TOURIST HOTEL FOR ISTANBUL, TURKEY

MOSQUES AND MINARETS, earlier native architecture of Istanbul, will one day soon be scenic contrast to the latest American-aided project in the East, the Istanbul Hilton Hotel, done by Skidmore, Owings & Merrill and their Turkish associate, Sedad H. Eldem.

In architectural terms, the mosques and the minarets have little more significance than ancient and revered landmarks in this or any other country. For something like twenty-five years the Turks have wanted, in fact made a point of rather demanding, international styles of architecture. Virtually all of the large buildings of recent years have been modern in concept and styling, something that could be said of perhaps no other country.

The new hotel will nevertheless represent a new high, literally as well as figuratively. It will be the highest building to date, and the most important, for it will become the focus of business and diplomatic (and tourist) functions and activities. Designwise, it will no doubt stand out for a quality of assertiveness, partly because this is one of the

Ezra Stoller

natural products of the American portion of the design association, partly because that quality is inherent in any of the new hotels beginning to dot the travel maps and posters.

In this instance, however, the scheme of the hotel departs from the strictly tourist concept, for it is to fill a larger need in Istanbul. This is essentially a project of the Turkish government, as are most of the later buildings there, and one of its purposes was to provide facilities for official functions. It is really a combination of the great tourist hotel and the hotel version of a palace.

This thinking is readily visible in the model photographs. The main shaft of the building contains the sleeping rooms, and follows the logical form of many strictly tourist hotels. The lower portion, however, is greatly extended, including all of the lounges, bars, restaurants and shops, flowing outward to pools and gardens and sports facilities of a vacation resort, but also having the banquet and conference rooms of a hotel catering to business and government activities.

These purposes found their way into the architectural expression, though the interpretation is much more natural than the listing of the purposes might imply. The slick efficiency of the hotel-room shaft is manifest, and the extension of the two public floors offers no denial of this note. There is perhaps a gayer or more gracious note in the gradual movement outward of the lower floors, and there are motifs of definitely Turkish origin, these being suitable for tourist or diplomat alike. The picturesque quality of Turkish artistry will find its place in the interiors, even though the tourists have to take cabs to see the minarets.

From its beginning the hotel project seemed to accumulate a great deal of official attention, and was finally blessed with high-level approbation. Istanbul (Turkish government) had long sought to interest

Owner: *Turkish Republic Pension Fund*
Advisor-Operator: *Hilton Hotels International*
Associated Architects: *Skidmore, Owings & Merrill*
Sedad H. Eldem
Partners in Charge: *William S. Brown, Coordination*
Gordon Bunshaft, Design

Ezra Stoller

ISTANBUL HILTON HOTEL

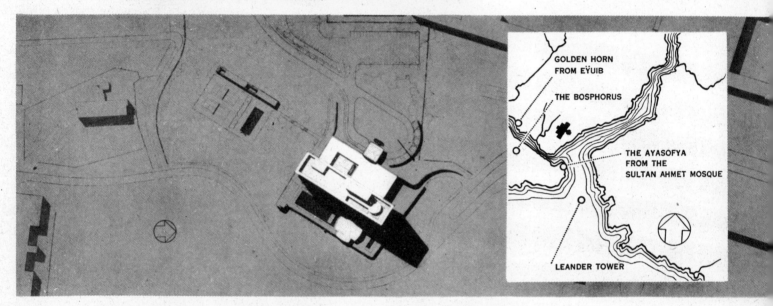

GOLDEN HORN
FROM EŸUIB

THE BOSPHORUS

THE AYASOFYA
FROM THE
SULTAN AHMET MOSQUE

LEANDER TOWER

For all of the European influences that have been felt in Turkey in its recent history, the country is still visited for historic scenic attractions. The hotel will have for its site a high hill overlooking the famous Bosporus (left, below). Within range of this hill (telescopic range, perhaps) are such views as the Leander Tower (left, above), the Golden Horn (opposite page) and the mosque d'Ayasofya (page 75)

Hotels International, and was subsequently assigned to the Turkish Republic Pension Fund for administration and for carrying out the provisions. The hotel will be operated under 20-year lease by Hilton Hotels International.

As a design assignment, the hotel had an unusual tie for Skidmore, Owings & Merrill, for the firm had previously been retained by the Turkish government to survey town planning, housing and building. Gordon Bunshaft, partner and design chief, had led a field group in a two-month trip through Turkey, culminating in a major set of recommendations to the Ministry of Public Works. The findings of the survey do not have too much bearing on this project, but the fact of the study did do much to smooth the planning procedures. Turkey does have much of modern technology, but like all Eastern cities is lacking in basic things like steel and cranes and tools and techniques.

Perhaps this hotel project will advance in some degree the firm's own recommendations about developing local industries. It is true that most of the materials will have to be brought in, but the project will have an unusual amount of participation by Turkish interests. Sedad Eldem, an award-winning contemporary architect, was an active participant in the early planning, spending many months in New York. Basic design was done in New York, also engineering. But working drawings were done in Istanbul by Eldem's office, with two S. O. & M. men working there for interpretations.

In design terms this is a normal project, affected by local shortages principally in steel-saving devices. The structural design, in reinforced concrete, was developed to use steel rods with exceptional economy. The structure will stand on continuous footing beams, with reinforcing rods carefully placed to match tension stresses, but designed without too much reliance on bonds. Beams throughout the building get over-sized, not only because of the steel saving, but also for an earthquake condition of second-degree magnitude.

The overall design takes full advantage of a site difficult to match in any of the tourist centers of the world. Bellevue Park, on the top portion of which the hotel will stand, is a high promontory overlooking the strategic Bosporus, with views and breezes to give the steamship and air lines much copy for their tourist folders.

Integration of indoors and outdoors, stressed so heavily in modern tourist hotels, is extensively but very naturally done. The upper (entrance) floor has an open patio in the center, surrounded by a group of shops on one side, main lobby on the other. Lobby opens on the other side to a very long cocktail terrace overlooking the garden, a modern version of the old front porch. Below, on the garden side the near visual focus is a reflecting pool, to be used also for skating. The hillside falls away rapidly toward a huge free-form swimming pool, with tennis courts and cabanas; farther still, to one side, is an amphitheater. And in the distance, those terrific views.

American capital in such a venture. ECA (now MSA) took an interest in this and other similar moves toward extension of commercial and tourist trade. An official tour was organized, with Conrad Hilton and John Houser of Hilton Hotels International, and Louis Skidmore and William Brown of the architectural firm, who visited London, Rome, Istanbul, Athens. Istanbul was the first city selected; there may be others. The enthusiastic cooperation of the Turkish government was a factor; funds and collaboration were made available. Also the choicest possible site; indeed the site is part of an ambitious park development for Istanbul, and but for official enthusiasm could not have been made available for any hotel, with or without international backing.

A contract with the Turkish government was signed by the Turkish minister of Foreign Affairs and Hilton

Ezra Stoller

The multiple purposes of the hotel show more plainly from the front entrance side; the great extension of the lower floor contains shops, offices, lounges, encircling an enclosed patio, with vast terrace hanging outward toward reflecting pool and gardens

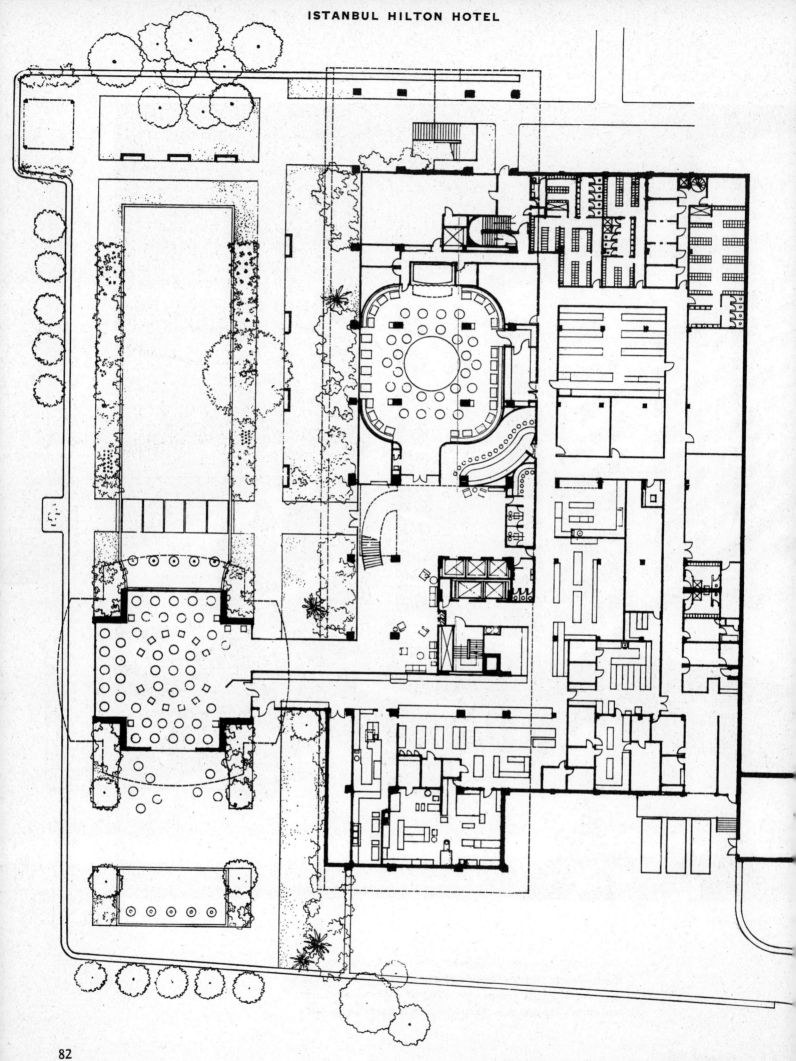

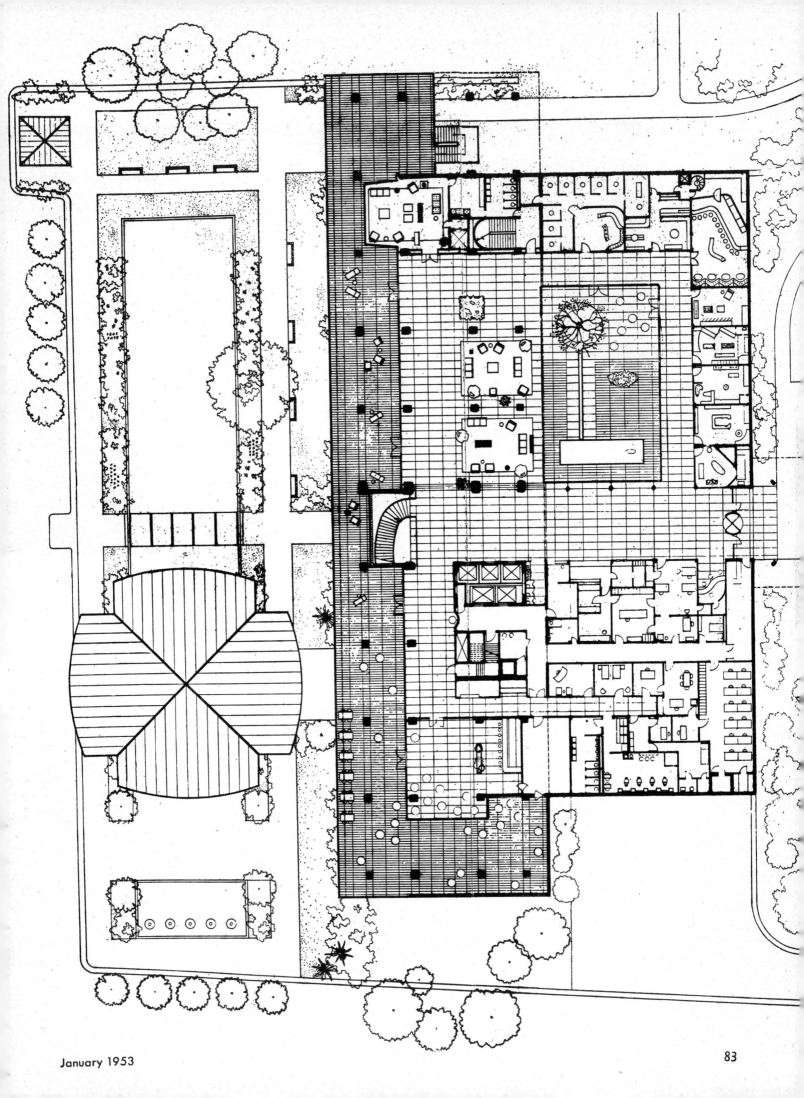

Viewed from this side the model gives a
better idea of the social and recreational
aspects of the hotel. Resort hotels have
gone through many changes, but the far-
away tourist hotel utilizes to the full the
"watering-place" development outdoors

Ezra Stoller

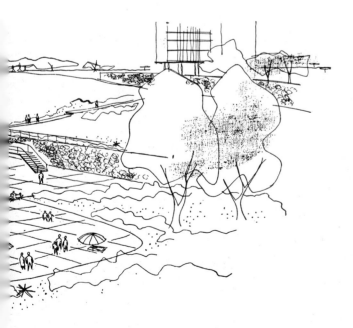

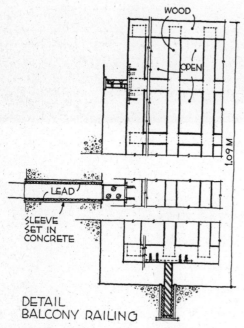

WOOD

OPEN

1.09 M

LEAD

SLEEVE
SET IN
CONCRETE

DETAIL
BALCONY RAILING

Each sleeping-room floor is identical, with all rooms alike except at the corners. A pent-house floor will have a few larger suites

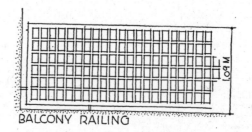

1.09 M

BALCONY RAILING

TYPICAL FLOOR PLAN

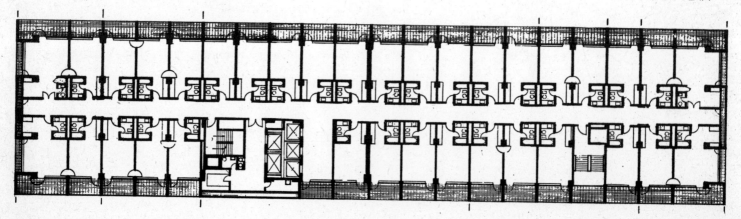

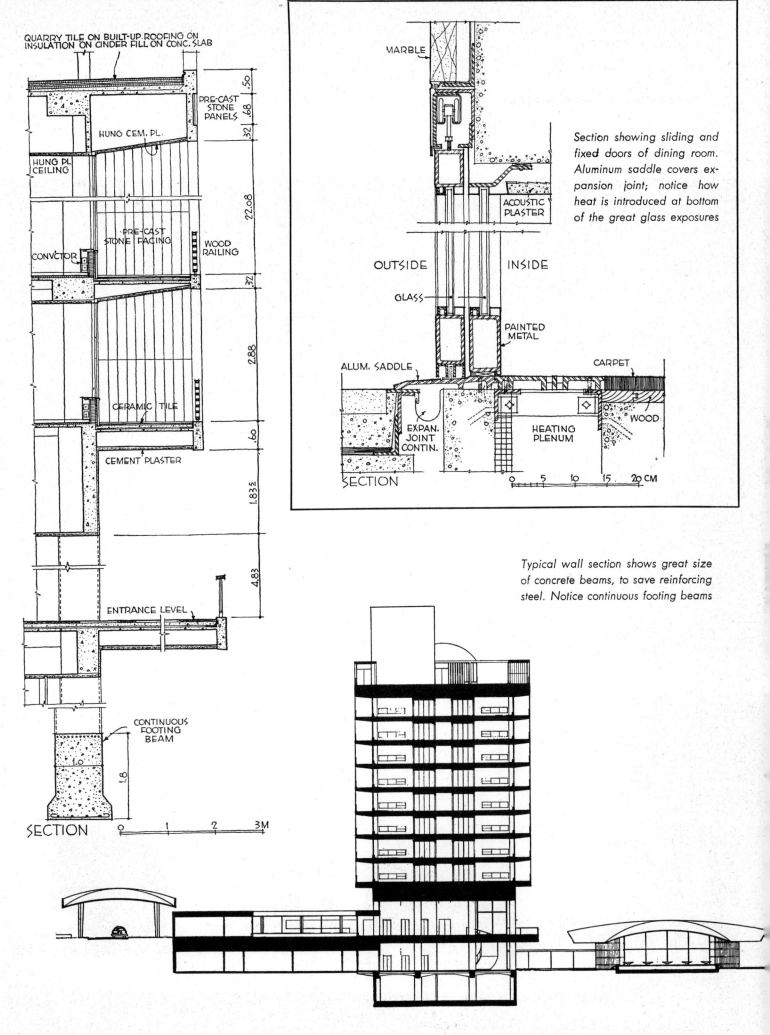

QUARRY TILE ON BUILT-UP ROOFING ON
INSULATION ON CINDER FILL ON CONC. SLAB

PRE-CAST STONE PANELS

HUNG CEM. PL.

HUNG PL CEILING

.50
.68
.32

CONV'CTOR

PRE-CAST STONE FACING

WOOD RAILING

22.08

CERAMIC TILE

.32

2.88

CEMENT PLASTER

.60

1.835

ENTRANCE LEVEL

4.83

CONTINUOUS FOOTING BEAM

1.0

1.8

SECTION

0 1 2 3M

MARBLE

Section showing sliding and
fixed doors of dining room.
Aluminum saddle covers expansion joint; notice how
heat is introduced at bottom
of the great glass exposures

ACOUSTIC PLASTER

OUTSIDE   INSIDE

GLASS

PAINTED METAL

ALUM. SADDLE

CARPET

WOOD

EXPAN. JOINT CONTIN.

HEATING PLENUM

SECTION

0 5 10 15 20 CM

Typical wall section shows great size
of concrete beams, to save reinforcing
steel. Notice continuous footing beams

ISTANBUL HILTON HOTEL

Ezra Stoller

STATLER CENTER

LOS ANGELES

Holabird & Root and Burgee

Architects and Engineers

William B. Tabler

Associate Architect

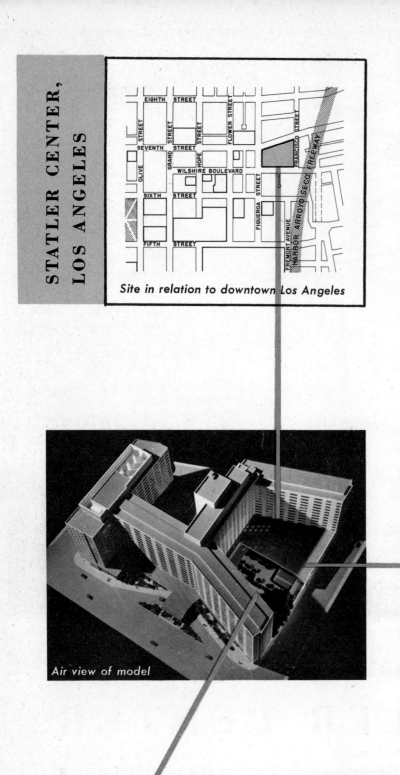

STATLER CENTER, LOS ANGELES

Site in relation to downtown Los Angeles

Air view of model

Schematic section showing garden court

Unique among commercial hotels, Statler Center in Los Angeles will be notable for its many types of accommodations and for the hospitably open character which its owners and designers have infused into it.

The east wing is to be a 13-story office building with 150,000 sq ft of rentable space; the hotel portion will have 1275 guest rooms; public areas will contain 70,000 sq ft of shops; in the basement is to be a 3-level garage. The decision to include all these facilities was made for reasons almost wholly economic.

The Statler organization's long experience at picking a proper city, and within that a suitable site, plus the architects' knowledge of their needs, led to selecting this particular location. Like Washington, Los Angeles was judged to need downtown convention, meeting, and display space. Office facilities in the older Boston Statler had long provided welcome extra revenue; Los Angeles needed office space; to put a complete office building on the very large plot entailed no additional expense for land, and the income from it would help defray the increasing cost of operating the hotel and its three spacious levels of public area.

There were other design determinants. Statler Center, Los Angeles, could not be just another big-city hotel, as appropriate for Chicago as for a semi-tropical metropolis. It must have openness and vegetation suitable for Southern California; hence its hotel wings will spread wide; a guest will scarcely be conscious of the space between them as a "court"; no bedroom window will face another window directly. Tropical planting will enhance all courts and main entrances.

The city, the Statler organization and the architects worked together through months of preliminary negotiations, each giving and taking by turns, to fit the Center into its locale. Hotel entrances from Wilshire Boulevard and Seventh St. have off-street driveways so lines of taxis will not block traffic. The design at first called for an off-street trucking dock and garage entrance from Seventh; this was rejected by the city as causing too much congestion on Seventh. The city is extending Francisco St. (which formerly stopped at Seventh), with Statler donating a strip of land 10 ft wide and the city condemning the remainder. Now garage and truck entrances are near the corner of Seventh and Francisco; and, with the new street, taxicabs can leave guests at the Seventh St. entrance, circle the Center and pick up fares at the Wilshire doors.

Height restrictions—thirteen stories above basements to a maximum of 165 ft, excluding penthouses—were another matter. To get into the Center the number of rooms required to insure success, and at the same time maintain a Californian openness, all the plot has had to be utilized. The entire Center is air conditioned from a Fan Gallery Mezzanine above the Ballroom level, from which conventional air supplies lead down to public areas and high velocity systems rise to offices and guest rooms.

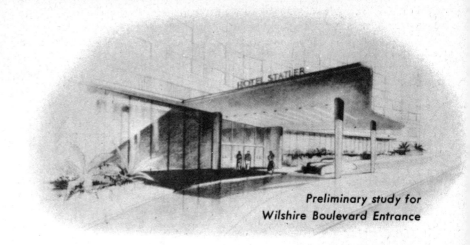

Preliminary study for
Wilshire Boulevard Entrance

Landscaped garden with pool
gives Cocktail Garden its name

Seventh Street Entrance is expected
to have heavy guest traffic

Indicated by the green band, above, are the three lower levels, only partly above grade, which contain all public areas

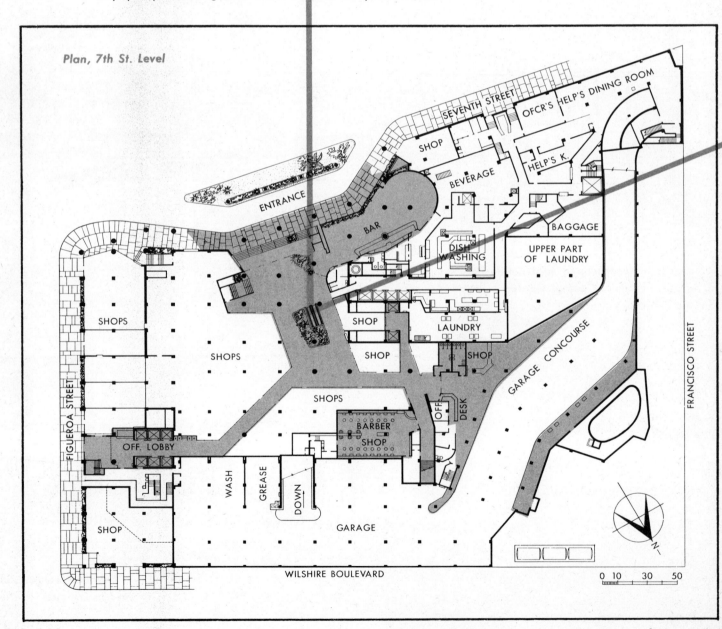

Plan, 7th St. Level

SEVENTH STREET

OFCR'S HELP'S DINING ROOM

SHOP

BEVERAGE

HELP'S K.

ENTRANCE

BAR

BAGGAGE

DISH WASHING

UPPER PART OF LAUNDRY

SHOPS

SHOP

SHOP

LAUNDRY

SHOP

SHOPS

GARAGE CONCOURSE

SHOPS

OFF.

DESK

BARBER SHOP

OFF. LOBBY

FIGUEROA STREET

FRANCISCO STREET

WASH

GREASE

DOWN

SHOP

GARAGE

WILSHIRE BOULEVARD

0 10 30 50

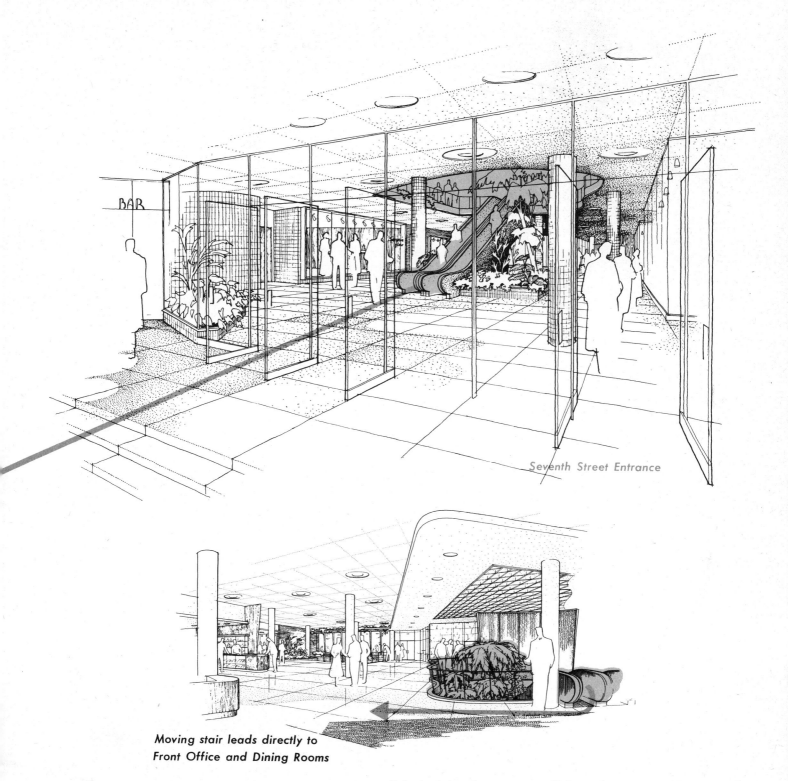

Seventh Street Entrance

Moving stair leads directly to
Front Office and Dining Rooms

Principal hotel entrances will have driveways so taxis
need not obstruct the thoroughfares; public sidewalks
curve in to follow the building wall. Most hotel guests
are expected to arrive via 7th St. Directly in front of
this entrance is to be a moving stair leading up through
a wide, invitingly planted well to the Front Office on
the level above. At the southwest corner of the building
is the garage entrance from which a drive ramps down
to three floors of parking space. Well worth noting is
the simplicity of circulation throughout the structure,
despite its complexity.

STATLER CENTER: WILSHIRE LEVEL

Like other public floors, the Wilshire level is organized around the garden (shown more fully on subsequent pages). Here also is a good share of the 70,000 sq ft of shop area, nearly all of which has street frontage as well as lobby show windows. Through the office building lobby there will be access from Figueroa St. as well as Wilshire. On the extension of Francisco St. at the west end of the site is to be the off-street loading dock, where supplies can be delivered to the kitchen on virtually one level; only for service to ballrooms and private dining rooms on the floor above, and for room service to hotel guests and office tenants, will food need to be transported vertically. This, plus the ingenious way in which dining areas are placed around the kitchen, will help to insure fast, efficient service.

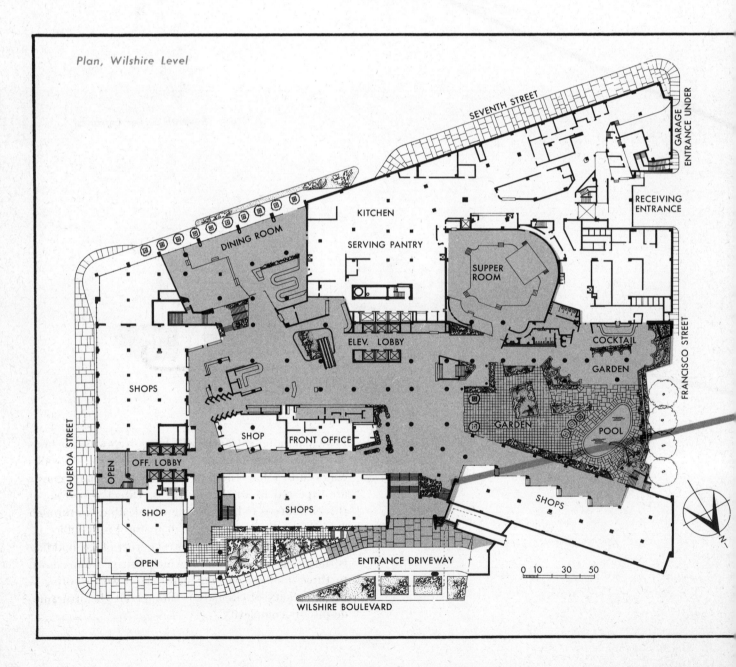

Plan, Wilshire Level

Main Dining Room

Open planning is not confined to wide spacing of the upper-story wings; at entrances, notably from Wilshire Boulevard, every effort is made to impress one with a hospitably open atmosphere. The most important stairs lead directly to the lobby which contains the front office, and from which dining rooms, Supper Room and Cocktail Garden are reached

Wilshire Entrance

Cocktail Garden

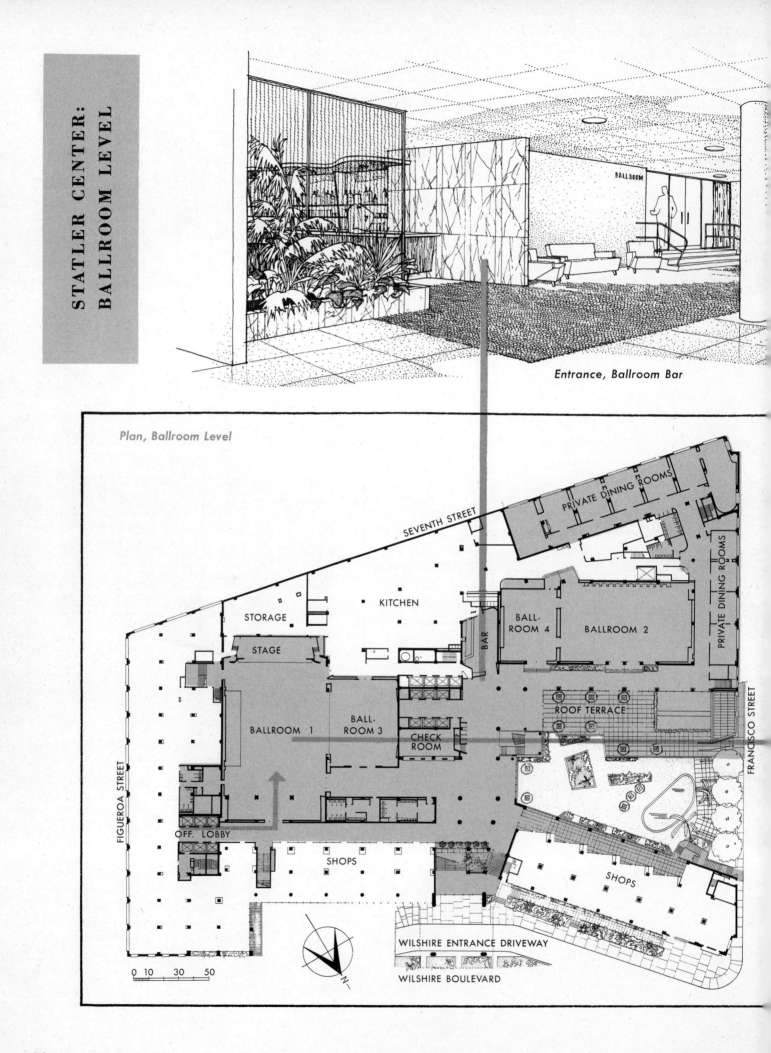

STATLER CENTER:
BALLROOM LEVEL

Entrance, Ballroom Bar

BALLROOM

Plan, Ballroom Level

SEVENTH STREET

PRIVATE DINING ROOMS

PRIVATE DINING ROOMS

KITCHEN

STORAGE

STAGE

BAR

BALL-
ROOM 4

BALLROOM 2

FRANCISCO STREET

ROOF TERRACE

BALLROOM 1

BALL-
ROOM 3

CHECK
ROOM

FIGUEROA STREET

OFF. LOBBY

SHOPS

SHOPS

0 10   30   50

WILSHIRE ENTRANCE DRIVEWAY

WILSHIRE BOULEVARD

N

Ballroom No. 3

In the past, ballrooms have often been placed at the top-most levels of hotels. In Statler Center they have been placed as close to ground level as possible, so that people not resident in the hotel can reach all public functions without either traversing guest room areas or burdening elevators. This simplifies traffic control and makes possible efficient elevator service at relatively low installation cost. Again, the conventional air conditioning required

Main Ballroom, No. 1

for public areas can all be supplied directly from the fan gallery immediately above; the short ducts need not cross guest room floors, which have separate supply systems. At Ballroom level the office building floor will serve as exhibition space for manufactured products. Hotel and office areas are interconnected at this level, making available to office tenants all function facilities of the hotel.

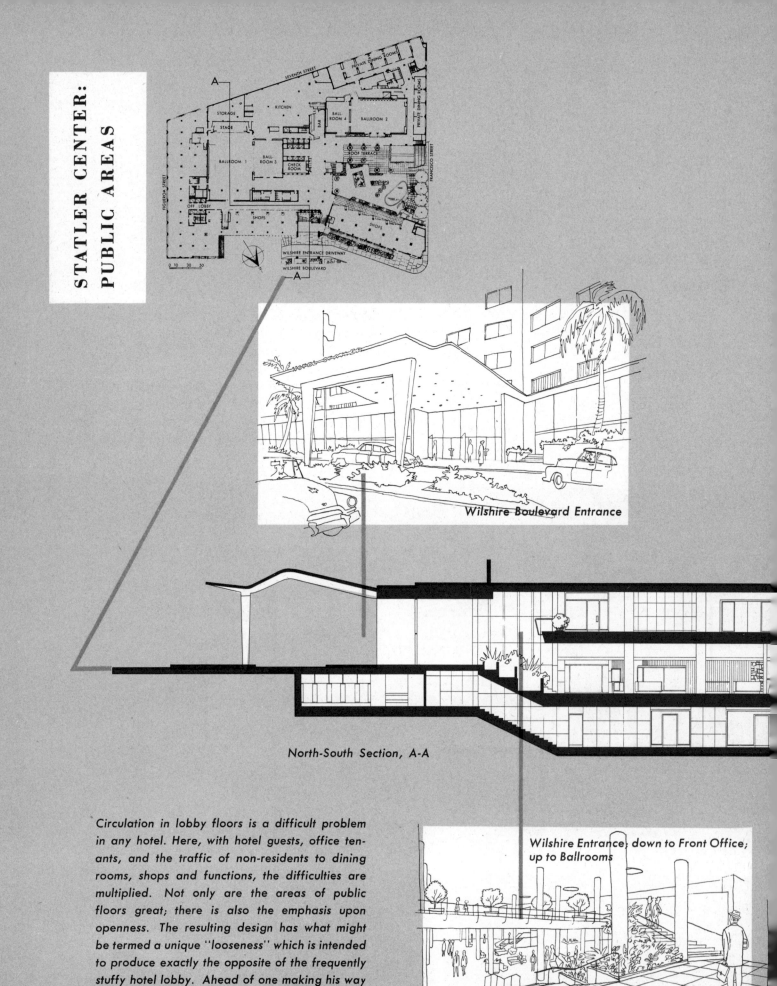

Wilshire Boulevard Entrance

North-South Section, A-A

Circulation in lobby floors is a difficult problem in any hotel. Here, with hotel guests, office tenants, and the traffic of non-residents to dining rooms, shops and functions, the difficulties are multiplied. Not only are the areas of public floors great; there is also the emphasis upon openness. The resulting design has what might be termed a unique "looseness" which is intended to produce exactly the opposite of the frequently stuffy hotel lobby. Ahead of one making his way through there will always be a vista enhanced by appropriate greenery; at the same time, certain landmarks will stand out to guide him

Wilshire Entrance: down to Front Office; up to Ballrooms

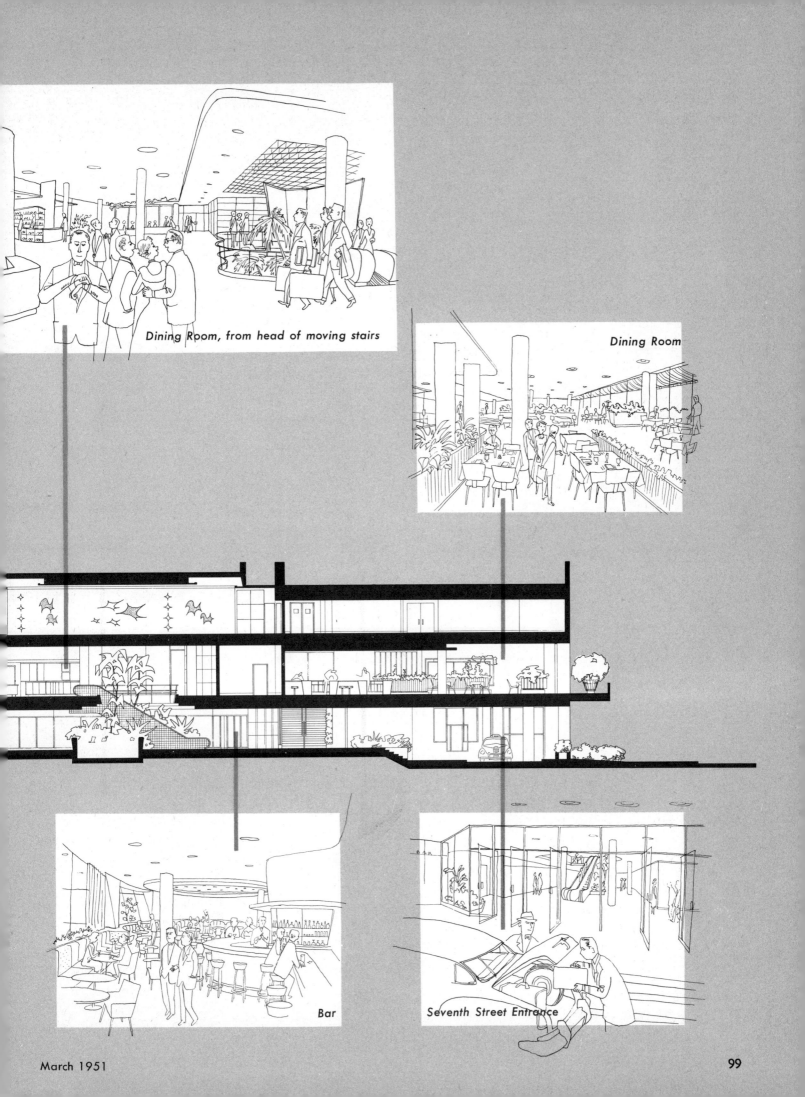

Dining Room, from head of moving stairs

Dining Room

Bar

Seventh Street Entrance

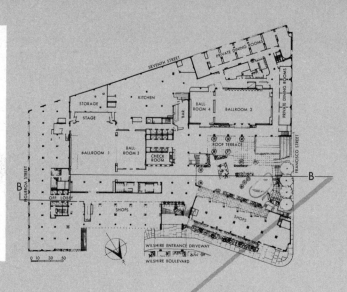

Ballroom Entrance

The East-West Section demonstrates the ingenuity with which the substantial difference in elevation of the surrounding streets has been turned to advantage. What might otherwise have only basement use has been transformed into a garden. Surrounded by glass walls, this becomes the feature around which planning of all public levels revolves

East-West Section, B-B

Cocktail Garden

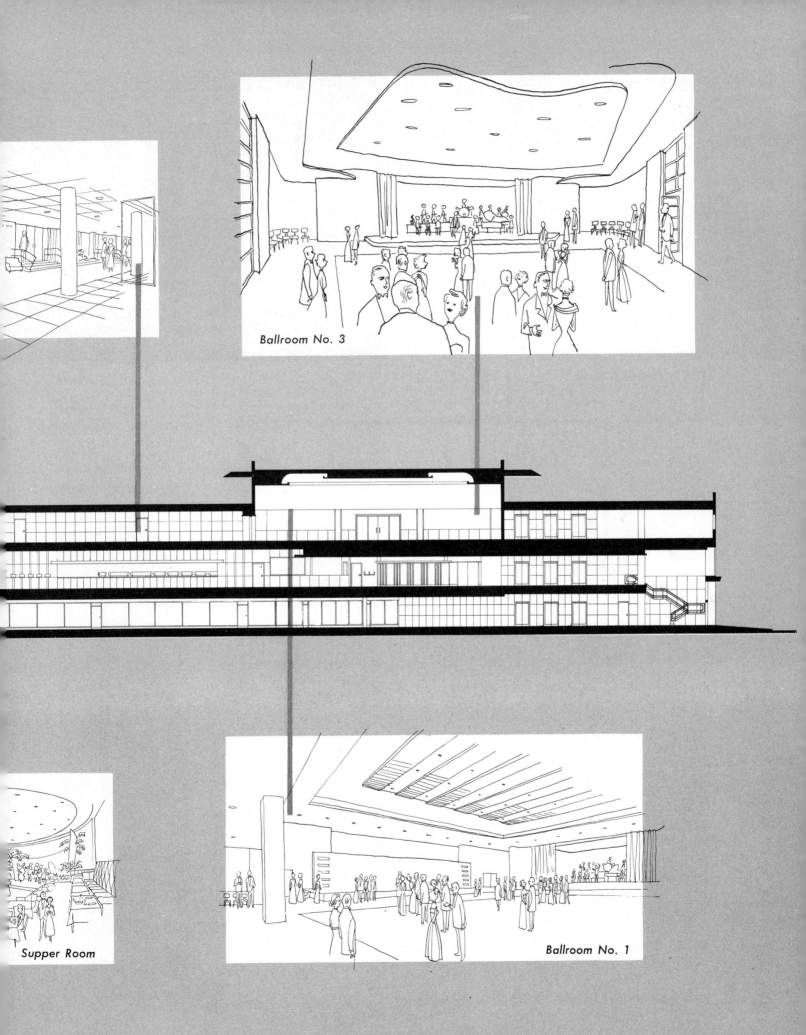

Ballroom No. 3

Supper Room

Ballroom No. 1

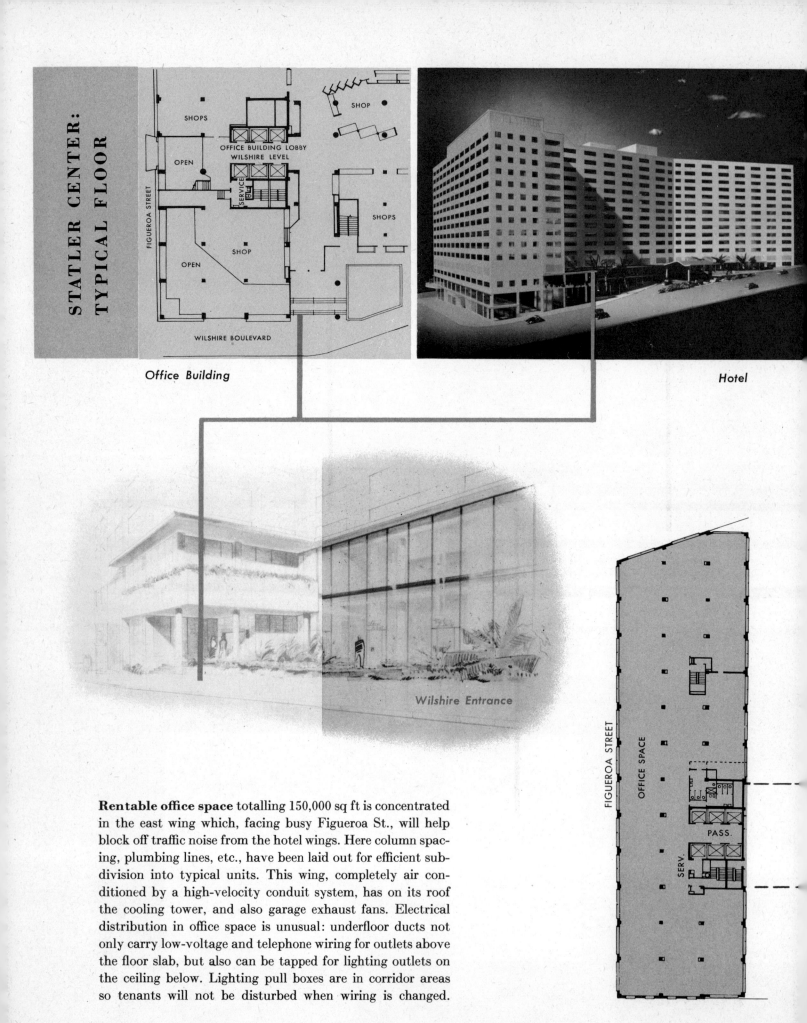

STATLER CENTER: TYPICAL FLOOR

SHOPS

SHOP

OPEN

OFFICE BUILDING LOBBY
WILSHIRE LEVEL

FIGUEROA STREET

SERVICE

OPEN

SHOP

SHOPS

WILSHIRE BOULEVARD

Office Building

Hotel

Wilshire Entrance

FIGUEROA STREET

OFFICE SPACE

PASS.

SERV.

Rentable office space totalling 150,000 sq ft is concentrated in the east wing which, facing busy Figueroa St., will help block off traffic noise from the hotel wings. Here column spacing, plumbing lines, etc., have been laid out for efficient subdivision into typical units. This wing, completely air conditioned by a high-velocity conduit system, has on its roof the cooling tower, and also garage exhaust fans. Electrical distribution in office space is unusual: underfloor ducts not only carry low-voltage and telephone wiring for outlets above the floor slab, but also can be tapped for lighting outlets on the ceiling below. Lighting pull boxes are in corridor areas so tenants will not be disturbed when wiring is changed.

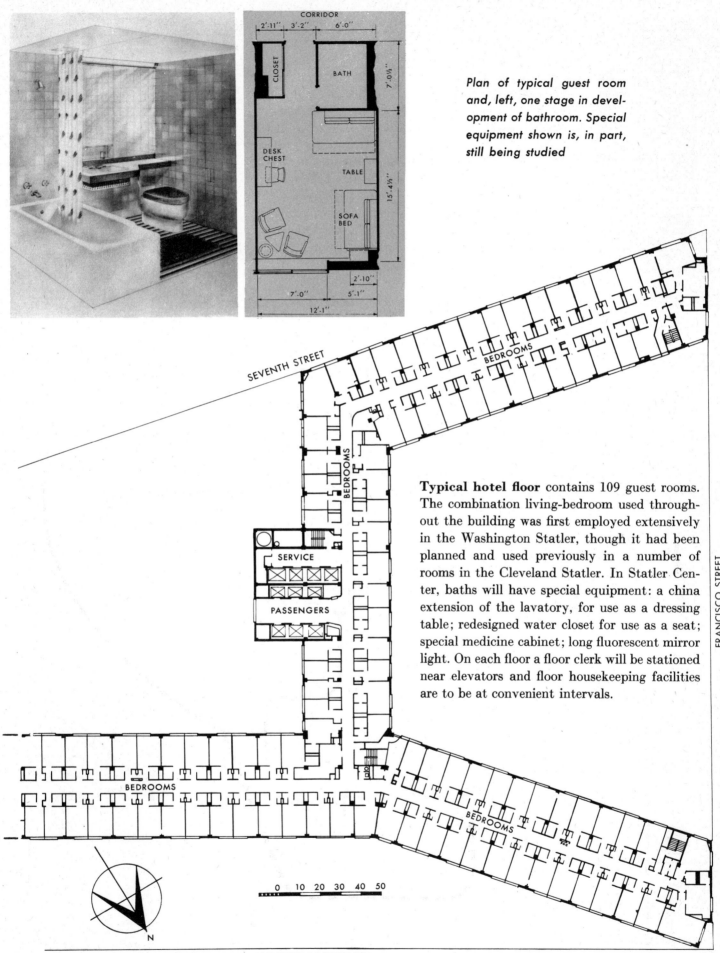

Plan of typical guest room
and, left, one stage in development of bathroom. Special
equipment shown is, in part,
still being studied

Typical hotel floor contains 109 guest rooms. The combination living-bedroom used throughout the building was first employed extensively in the Washington Statler, though it had been planned and used previously in a number of rooms in the Cleveland Statler. In Statler Center, baths will have special equipment: a china extension of the lavatory, for use as a dressing table; redesigned water closet for use as a seat; special medicine cabinet; long fluorescent mirror light. On each floor a floor clerk will be stationed near elevators and floor housekeeping facilities are to be at convenient intervals.

STATLER CENTER: GARAGE

The Parking Garage, like the off-street loading docks a city requirement, is to occupy most of three basement floors. If the clients and architects had been willing both to sacrifice some upper-level facilities and to accept a less open general scheme, or if restrictions had not limited the hotel's height, the several-hundred-car space might have been built above grade. Underground, the garage needs elaborate ventilation and sprinkler systems. On the other hand, grade-level space can realize greater income than a garage would produce. After such matters were weighed the basement garage was decided upon. A travel-weary guest arriving by car will not realize this; he can drive in, turn his car over to an attendant, register at a desk almost as he steps out, and proceed by special elevator directly to his room without traversing the main lobby.

This presentation in *Architectural Record* for March 1951, appearing also in the April 1951 issue of *Hotel Management*, was prepared in collaboration with the architects and the staff of Hotels Statler Co., Inc. Members of the Statler organization who were concerned with design of the Statler Center include: Harold B. Callis, Senior Vice President and Secretary, Hotels Statler Co., Inc.; Kenneth M. McCann, Vice President, Hotels Statler Co., Inc., Vice President and General Manager, Statler Studios, Inc.; Fred E. Smith, Asst. Vice Pres., Statler Studios, Inc.; W. Randolph Leber, Asst. Vice Pres., Executive Engineer, Hotels Statler Co., Inc.; Edward Podmayer, Asst. to Mr. Leber; Ernest Wottitz, Architect, Chief Designer; I. Noel Simon, Staff Architect; Helen McQuillan, Staff Decorator.

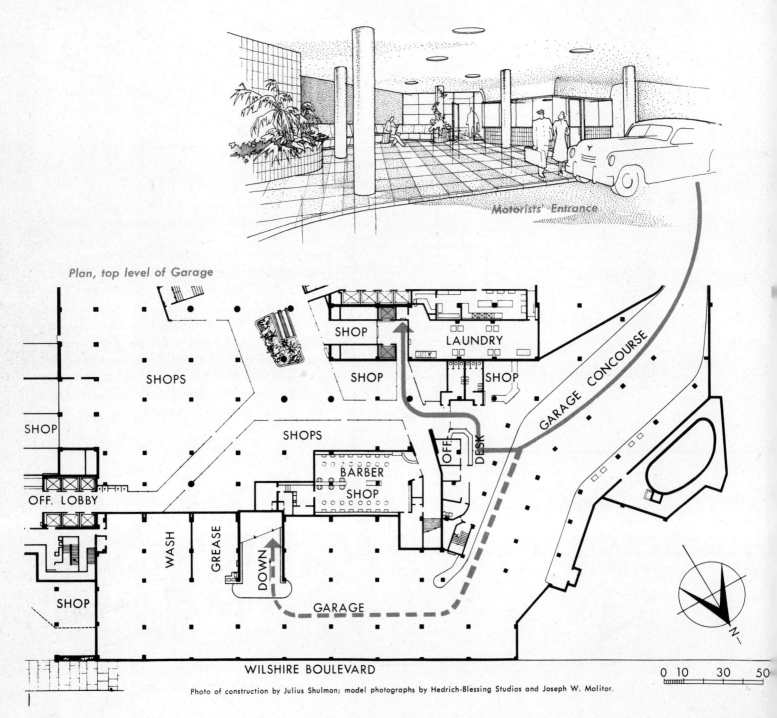

Motorists' Entrance

Plan, top level of Garage

SHOP
SHOPS
SHOP
SHOP
LAUNDRY
SHOP
SHOP
OFF. LOBBY
SHOPS
OFF.
DESK
GARAGE CONCOURSE
BARBER SHOP
WASH
GREASE
DOWN
SHOP
GARAGE
WILSHIRE BOULEVARD

0 10   30   50

Photo of construction by Julius Shulman; model photographs by Hedrich-Blessing Studios and Joseph W. Molitor.

STATLER CENTER

LOS ANGELES

Holabird & Root & Burgee

Architects and Engineers

William B. Tabler

Associate Architect

Julius Shulman

On August 6, 1952, the first few floors of guest rooms in the Los Angeles Statler were opened. Some weeks before, tenants had begun moving into the Center's office building wing. On October 27 the entire Center was formally dedicated. Constructing and equipping this hotel project — the largest built in the United States in more than 20 years — took a little over two years; construction started July 5, 1950. Preceding even this date were an exhaustive analysis of the needs and potentialities of Los Angeles as a city in which Hotels Statler Company would be prepared to invest some $25,000,000; selection of the 3-acre site, twice as large as that of the 1943 Washington Statler; and determination of a program which took into account the Statler budget, rising construction costs, building and zoning regulations, site and traffic conditions, desirable allocations of cubic contents and square footage to the various purposes, and above all the number, type, size and arrangements of the guest rooms which remain relatively the most profitable part of any hotel.

Following the programming, design proceeded through a number of preliminary stages. At one point it was found that, considering trends in operating and maintenance costs, a building designed solely as a hotel might not produce adequate profit at room rates in keeping with Statler policy. Since the Company had had experience with rental office space at its Boston hotel, the decision to include an office building on the large Los Angeles site was comparatively easy to make.

The program aimed at 1300 guest rooms; as built, the Center contains 1275, 70 per cent of them studio twin bed rooms refined from the Washington Statler precedent. These occupy 52 per cent of the cubic contents of the Center's hotel portion; function and public rooms, hotel offices, services, mechanical plant, etc., occupy the other 48 per cent. Net area per hotel floor devoted to guest rooms is 53 per cent of the gross, compared with 47 per cent in the Washington Statler. It was early decided that Los Angeles needed public and service areas comparable to those provided in Washington; the new Center has more square footage but only five per cent more cubic content. Likewise,

Julius Shulman

70,000 sq ft of shops were provided; the subterranean garage has space for 465 cars, with a supplementary check-in desk and elevators so travel-weary motorists can go directly from their automobiles to guest rooms without traversing public areas. The office building wing contains 150,000 sq ft of rentable area. Total content of the structure is 12,206,000 cu ft. For the entire Center, the contract cost was within estimates made three years earlier although construction prices had meanwhile increased 12 per cent.

Photo at top left shows the office building portion on busy Figueroa Street, convenient to other commercial areas of the city, and placed on the Center's site to shield the hotel portion from the noise of traffic and commerce. At top right is the Wilshire Boulevard side which provides a suitable "address" but, due to traffic conditions, is less convenient for most arriving guests than the opposite (Seventh St.) side. At right, high point of the sharply sloping sight, corner of Wilshire and a new street, Francisco, provided by the city on land partly donated by Statler.

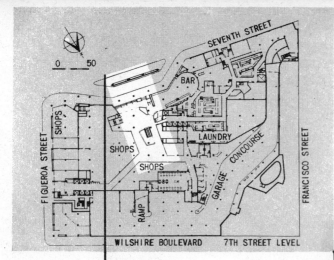

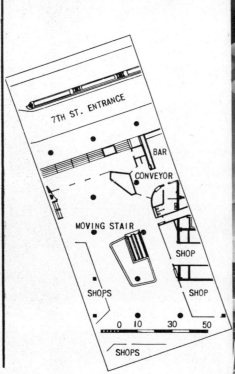

STATLER CENTER: PUBLIC AREAS

The sloping site permitted placing much of the extensive shop area at the various street levels and facilitated arrangement of public space on the three main floors (see earlier article pages 89 through 104). Interior design is here no superficial matter of finishes and furniture. It is all-important and three-dimensional. For entering guests, circulation is direct. Tenants from the office building find convenient passages to dining rooms apart from the guest lobby. Conventioneers, drawn by the gay garden, cocktail lounge, supper club and promenades, find themselves mounting a prominent stair to ballrooms above. Behind the successfully brilliant mosaic mural (top photo) is the elevator lobby, located so that it cannot become a passageway.

Mosaic mural: Max Spivak

Julius Shulman

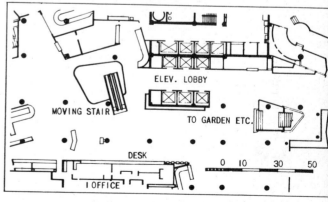

ELEV. LOBBY

MOVING STAIR

TO GARDEN ETC.

DESK

OFFICE

0   10   30   50

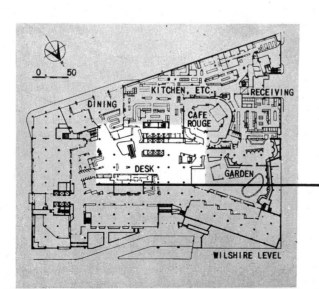

0   50

KITCHEN, ETC.

DINING

RECEIVING

CAFE ROUGE

DESK

GARDEN

WILSHIRE LEVEL

Most guests reach Wilshire level (left) by moving stair (above); on arrival they face desk with business section to one side, garden and public rooms on other

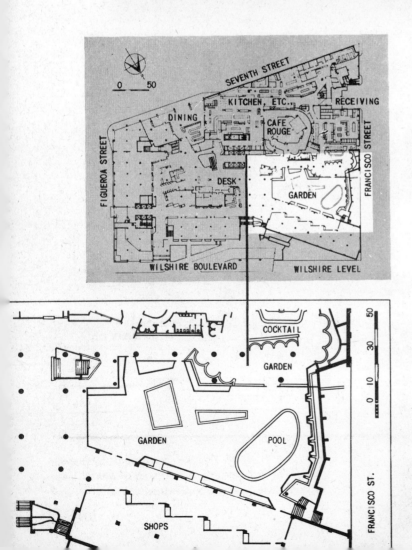

Clustered around the garden in the court which separates the north and south hotel wings are several public areas. To the east the garden is protected by the planted retaining wall that supports Francisco Street and by the street itself, from the possible encroachment of future buildings. Photos: far left, view from stair to ballrooms;

Julius Shulman

left, across garden pool toward two-story promenade and shops; above, on the promenade; right, garden stair. Below, left, Veranda Cafe and cocktail lounge; and right, from roof terrace above Veranda Cafe. Brightly lighted at night, the garden might some day be a setting for a spectacular show or aquacade.

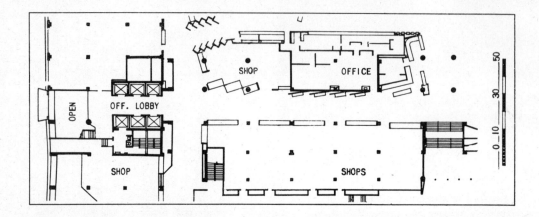

At top of page are, left, Cafe Rouge (popular priced dining room), divided into intimate sections by wood screens, plant boxes, color treatment and changes in level; center, Golden State Room, and right, Pacific Ballroom, two of the four ballrooms and eleven private dining rooms, all on one floor, and all served from one kitchen. Function facilities of the Statler Center are booked solid for many months. Pacific Ballroom in conjunction with adjoining Sierra Room can accommodate 1200 at a banquet when soundproof partition between them is raised. A small bar on this floor has proved extremely profitable.

Many shops in the Statler Center were designed by independent architects for individual tenants. Left below, cases project into the hotel lobby to provide profitable merchandising space. Right, sliding panels open another shop to corridor leading to the office building; airline ticket offices in background

PUBLIC ROOMS, SHOPS, OFFICES

Julius Shulman

Above, tenth-floor office building elevator lobby forms reception area for the Foote, Cone and Belding advertising agency. Left, looking down corridor from office building toward hotel lobby; airline offices at right of picture

a   b

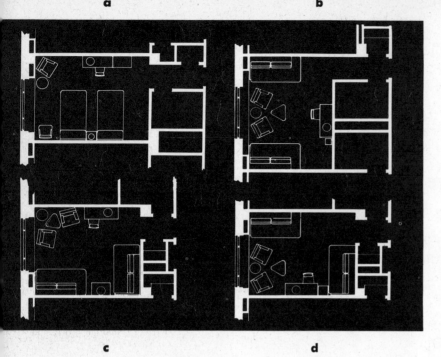

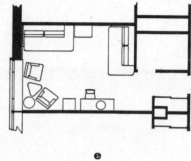

e

c   d

STATLER CENTER: GUEST ROOMS

SEVENTH STREET

FRANCISCO STREET

FIGUEROA STREET

RENTABLE OFFICE SPACE

SERVICE
PASSENGER

0   50

WILSHIRE BOULEVARD   4-15TH FLOORS

Evolution of the studio type of guest room used for 70 per cent of the rooms in the Los Angeles Statler. While this had been used in the Company's Cleveland and Detroit hotels in the late 1930's, its first extensive use was in the Washington Statler in 1943. The conventional guest room (a) 11 to 12 ft wide, had furniture so placed that rooms were full of beds, floor space broken into ineffective small areas. Spreading beds apart unified these areas. The room was turned 90 degrees (b); it became logical to make beds convertible to couches for daytime living, meetings, etc., and the public response was so great that very few of the so-called conventional rooms were used in Los Angeles. Variations c and d were used in Washington. Los Angeles rooms are slightly larger, have specially designed sofa-beds, more economical bath and closet arrangement in several variants of plan e. Since a solid wall is needed to prevent down-draft on one bed, interior design influenced fenestration and exterior appearance. Note also special bathroom vanity-lavatory and seat placement, photo left, below

Julius Shulman

NEW HOTEL FOR THE CARIBBEAN

Harold Sterner, Architect

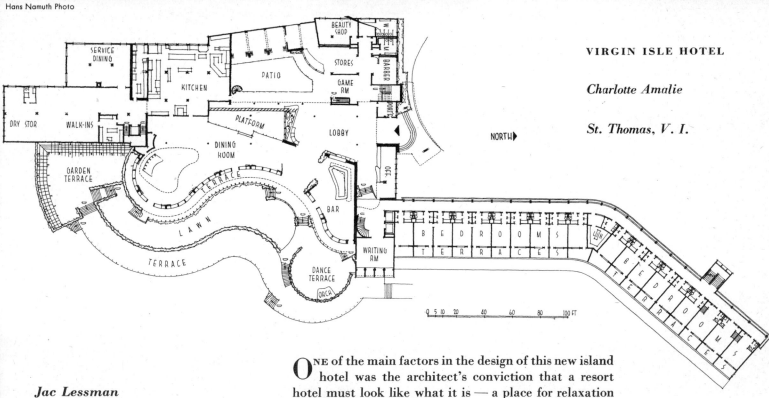

Hans Namuth Photo

VIRGIN ISLE HOTEL

Charlotte Amalie

St. Thomas, V. I.

Jac Lessman

Associate Designer

Virgin Islands Construction Co., Inc.

General Contractor

ONE of the main factors in the design of this new island hotel was the architect's conviction that a resort hotel must look like what it is — a place for relaxation and fun. Wide and curving terraces, a sweeping entrance canopy, continuous balconies and a kidney-shaped swimming pool combine to make the character of the building easily recognized from sea or air.

A second major design factor was the island's climate. The building is located on a spur running almost due north-south. Since the very welcome prevailing winds are roughly east-northeast, bedrooms are all on one side of a long, narrow wing following the line of the spur. Main public rooms also face in a general easterly direction.

Original plans called for a modest 30-room structure, with the bedroom wing only three stories in height.

Subsequent expansion, after construction had started, brought the hotel up to its present size, and incidentally increased the general informality of the plan.

Construction is reinforced concrete and concrete frame with 8-in. block bearing walls. Interior partitions are cement block, floors are slab tile with terrazzo finish.

Hans Namuth Photos

Swimming pool and terraces are the main features of the hotel. The two lower floors of the south wing are lined with cabanas on the pool side; above them (plan, page 115) are dining room, bar, dance terrace. Main entrance (below) is at north side of main wing, at third-floor level. Corridors in bedroom wing (bottom, opposite) are open

Hans Namuth Photos

Above: steps leading up to dance terrace past the glassed-in bar. Right: the main dining room. Trade winds are sufficiently strong at mid-day peak to require glassing-in of such areas despite the mild climate

Above, left: main lobby, like other public areas, is large and airy, with open terrace only a few feet away. Above, right: the garden terrace, on south side of main wing, is well sheltered from trade winds. Below: every bedroom has its own terrace overlooking the harbor, and its own short-wave radio set; several duplex two-room suites are provided at northernmost end of wing. Furnishings throughout are mahogany and native fabrics

GOLDEN STRAND HOTEL

Miami Beach, Fla.

Igor B. Polevitzky, Architect

Richard A. Belsham, Structural Engineer

Frederick B. Stressau, Landscape Architect

RESORT HOTELS are expected to be luxurious, and this new one at Miami Beach really is. Consisting of two five-story buildings and 16 small villas, it has its own beach, boardwalk, shuffleboard court, cabanas with hot and cold water, and a salt-water pool 40 ft wide and 82 ft long equipped for a complete water change every four hours. Every hotel apartment has a private terrace overlooking the ocean; each villa has a screened patio with a view of the ocean; and all rooms throughout the development have cross ventilation.

The two larger buildings have complete hotel facilities including dining rooms, bar, barber and beauty shops and drug store; many of the suites have kitchens. The villas are all two-bedroom, with fully equipped kitchens and separate service entrances, large living-dining areas, and two baths.

The deep site, stretching from the street back to a private beach, has been carefully planned for maximum use and maximum privacy. The two five-story buildings at the front serve as office and reception area. The villas behind them are arranged so that each has a view of the ocean and a private lawn. The beach is flanked by attendants' quarters

Rudi Rada: Pictor

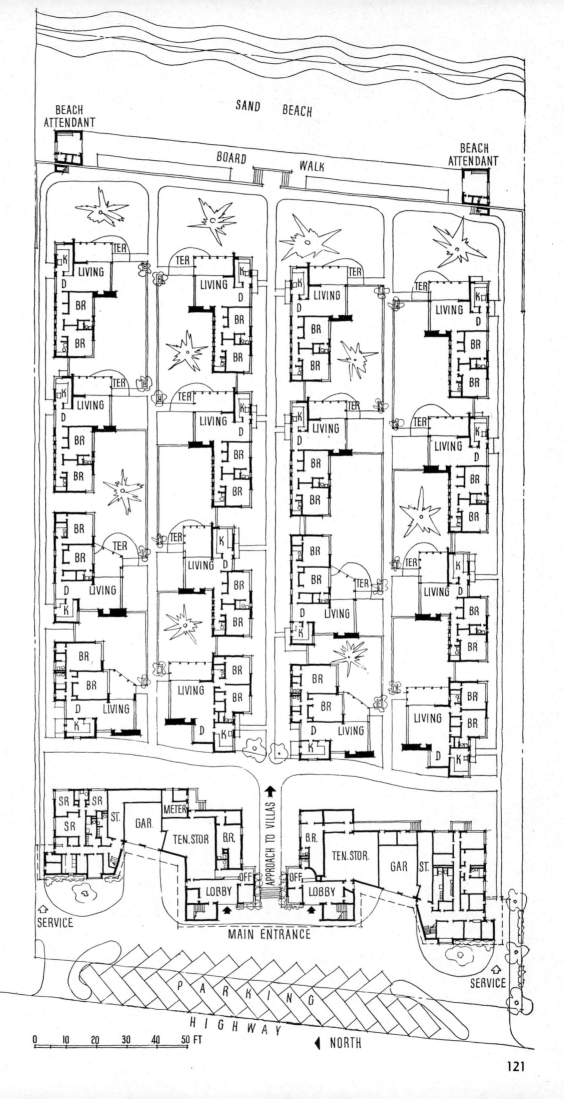

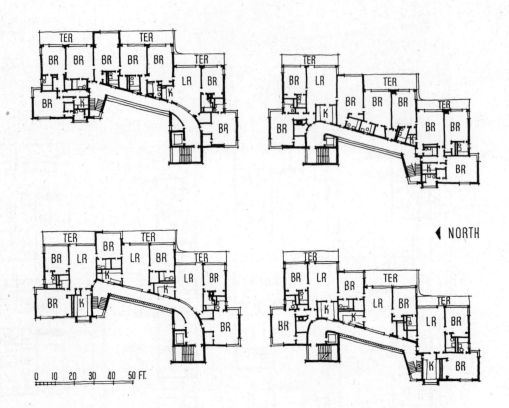

◄ NORTH

0 10 20 30 40 50 FT.

The twin buildings of the hotel proper offer various types of accommodation, including two-bedroom suites with living room and
kitchen. Plans above are of second and third floors (lower plan)
and fourth and fifth floors (upper plan). Below, left: bar and
cocktail lounge, looking toward main dining room. Below, right:
a typical bedroom in hotel proper, showing balcony in center rear

Rudi Rada: Pictor

The villas are all free-standing one-story cottages with
good kitchens and ample living space. Four of them (above)
front directly on the ocean. Below: typical villa interiors

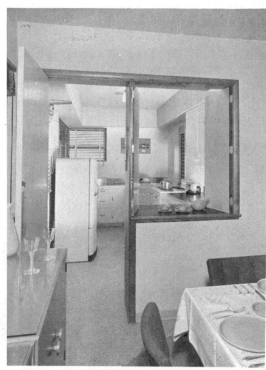

SEASIDE HOTEL IS REMODELED

Dune Deck Hotel, Westhampton, Long Island   **William Lescaze, Architect**

Extensive remodeling, which included an addition to the existing structure, has turned a formerly drab looking hotel into an attractive summer resort. Located on a broad sandspit separating the Atlantic Ocean from Moriches Bay on Long Island's south shore, the hotel needed an enlarged boardwalk, additional dining space and the transfer of the kitchen to the second floor — adjacent to the dining rooms. The entrance from the parking area was freshly treated — blending the old and the new in such a way as to create a harmonious balance (lower left photo, opposite page). Douglas fir

has been used for framing; interior walls are plywood; floors in lobby and cocktail lounge are cork. Horizontal sliding windows in three walls of the dining room provide excellent ventilation and light and give a view from all parts of the room. An outdoor dining terrace on a section of the boardwalk is partially protected by the overhanging new addition to the building. Interior furnishings are contemporary Swedish designs made in this country.

Future plans call for remodeling of sleeping quarters. located in another wing of the building.

Illustration at left shows the hotel as it looked before remodeling—a bleak and cold structure, as compared with the new and improved façade that it now boasts. Entrance from parking area (opposite) unites the old and the new with a simply balanced grace

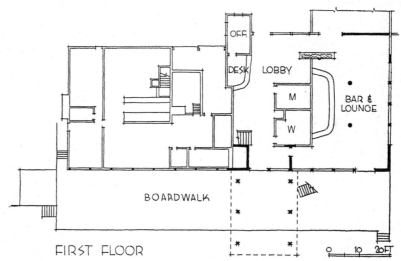

FIRST FLOOR

Labels: OFF. / DESK / LOBBY / M / W / BAR & LOUNGE / BOARDWALK

0   10   20FT

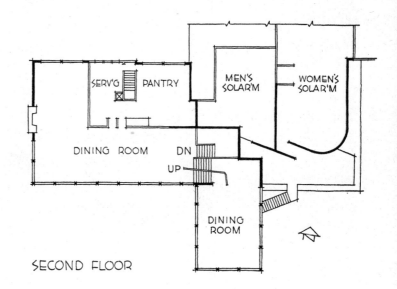

SECOND FLOOR

Labels: SERV'G PANTRY / MEN'S SOLAR'M / WOMEN'S SOLAR'M / DINING ROOM / DN / UP / DINING ROOM

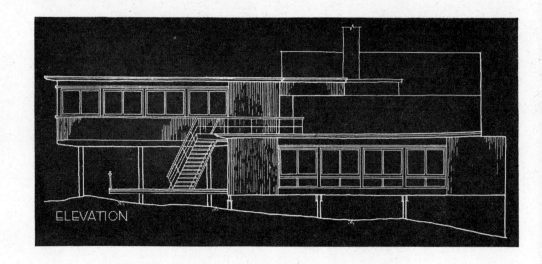

ELEVATION

Elevation above shows details of suspended dining room addition over boardwalk. Sliding glass windows in cocktail lounge and new dining room enhance view and provide excellent ventilation

Joseph W. Molitor

Left: steps leading from dining terrace on boardwalk to sun-bathing areas on upper deck. Entrance to lobby and cocktail lounge is through glass doors

Lobby, above, facing entrance from parking area. Entry to both dining
rooms is by stairway at left. Cocktail lounge is to right of lobby

New dining room, above, overlooks ocean; has sliding glass windows
on three walls. Bar, below, is accessible to outdoor dining terrace

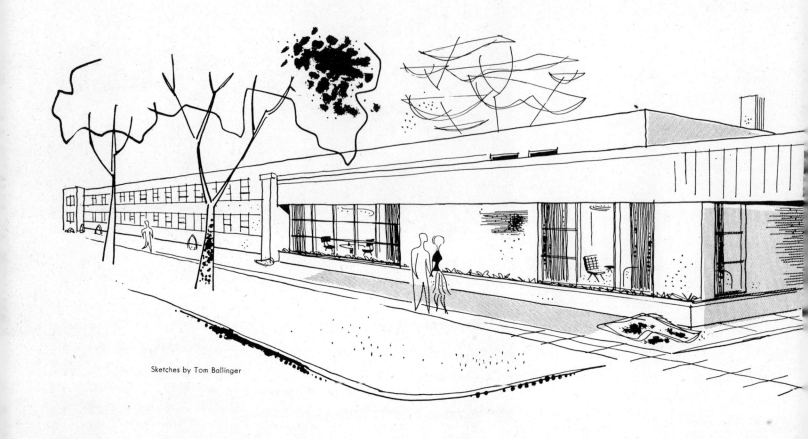

Sketches by Tom Ballinger

WISCONSIN HOTEL

Neatly designed Hotel Mead is planned for convenience of motorists, is run similar to motel

Hotel Mead, Wisconsin Rapids, Wis.

Donn Hougen, Architect

PROVIDES MOTEL FACILITIES

SINCE THE TOURIST COURT first made its appearance in outlying city areas, there has been a mounting concern among hotel planners and operators over the benefits that the courts, and the larger motels, offer automobile travelers: ample parking space, informality, no tipping. On the other hand, the downtown hotel still has certain advantages, especially for businessmen. The location is closer to business contacts, phone service is generally better, and meals and personal services are readily available if desired. Now we have a new concept, a "motelized hotel" which seeks to combine the features of both.

The new Mead Hotel was specifically designed to replace an older Wisconsin Rapids hotel, which is being torn down to make a place for a public park. Its "motelized" scheme was evolved after a survey of the area indicated that about 85 per cent of the hotel guests arrive by automobile. Throughout the project, the architect worked in close conjunction with the engineers and executives of the Consolidated Water Power and Paper Co., owners of the hotel.

The site chosen for the building is on one of the main highways running through the community, and is located a short distance from the actual downtown business area. The plot layout provides access from the principal street through a covered drive flanking the lobby; the building entrance is set well back from the street to cut down traffic hazards. The parking lot is at the rear with exits on a minor street.

The building itself was planned with two floors of guest rooms flanking a central corridor. Three entrances from the parking lot minimize the distance from car to room. Public rooms — dining room, bar and lobby — are grouped by the front office. The building is constructed of steel, concrete and masonry, and is radiant-heated by wrought iron coils in the first floor slab, copper coils in the second floor ceiling. All public areas are air conditioned, and corridors are pressurized by air conditioned units to provide a supply of filtered air to guest rooms. Acoustical plaster, carpeting, and painted cinder block corridor walls are used to cut down noise throughout the building.

Circulation for hotel guests is carefully worked out. From main highway, guest drives under canopy to front entrance. Long drive is heated, shelters several cars. At front office, guest is assigned key, parking place by rear entrance nearest his room. Desk has 24 hour service. After parking, the guest carries own luggage to first or second floor room. Same key unlocks outside door and room. All 84 rooms have baths, outside exposure; interiors are simple, comfortable, have multi-purpose desk-dressers. Parking area exits on secondary street to rear; guest needn't return to lobby until he checks out

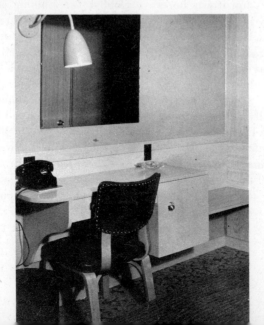

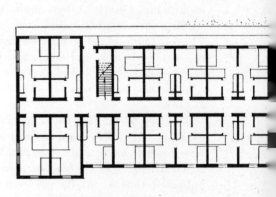

5 0 5 10 15 20 25 30 FT.

Second floor guestroom plan is identical to first (below), with manager's apartment at right. A basement is under lobby, dining and kitchen area, and houses heating system, food preparation and storage rooms, employees' lockers

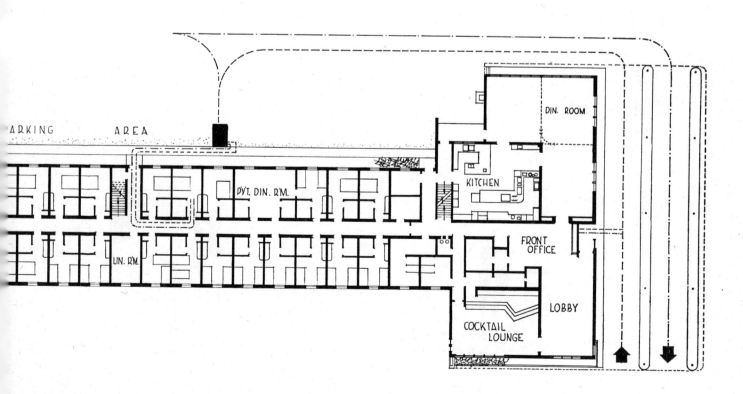

All public and service rooms are grouped at the entrance end of the building for easy supervision, and for convenient access by both hotel guests and community residents. Lobby, dining room and bar are all designed with numerous windows overlooking the quiet residential neighborhood. As in the guest rooms, interiors are kept simple, unobtrusive, comfortable. The dining room has an L-shaped plan and folding partitions, so that it can be divided in several ways to accommodate club and community groups as well as hotel guests. A small private dining room down the hall from the kitchen is planned for conversion into two extra guest rooms when needed. Plastic laminates are used extensively throughout the building to simplify upkeep. Such surfaces include counter, desk and table tops, bathroom walls, door surfaces, bed headboards and upholstery.

Sketches by Tom Ballinger

RESTAURANTS AND BARS

Gottscho-Schleisner Photos

NANTUCKET AT RADIO CITY

Gloucester House, West 51st Street, New York City

Francis Keally, Architect

ALTHOUGH New York City never, in our recollection, possessed a restaurant built in the shape of an oversized concrete hat, it does boast a seafood place designed to resemble an aquarium and another with swaying portholes intended, evidently, to test the seaworthiness of its customers at critical dietetic moments. Gloucester House, by comparison, is a staid and conservative Inn. While some architects might question the validity of constructing a Nantucket seafood place at the foot of the steel and glass towers of Radio City, there are probably good and sufficient business reasons for doing just that. The architect and the owner, at any rate, assured themselves of the validity of this approach after several weeks of detailed research, observation and investigation of the restaurant situation within a radius of ten city blocks of the proposed site. What they saw convinced them that their approach was right.

As an example of restaurant-design procedure, Gloucester House is extremely interesting. Not only was the architect called in to help decide the design, character and name of the restaurant, but he also controlled to a high degree such apparent incidentals as the layout of the menu cards and of the customers' checks, and helped style the waitresses' uniforms. Whether he helped select the waitresses as well we do not know. In any case, the result of such total architect-control is a very pleasing unity that pervades the entire design of this seafood restaurant.

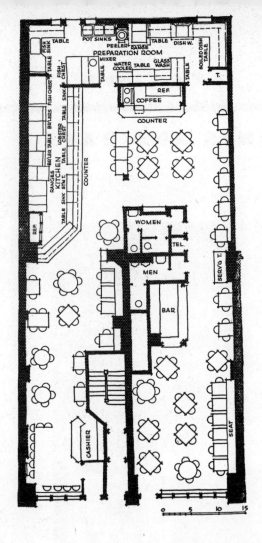

Existing conditions have helped to divide this restaurant into several intimate dining rooms. The efficient, handsomely tiled kitchen is visible to the customers. Lighting throughout uses filament lamps set into chandeliers constructed of cork floats (which should give a good account of themselves in a typhoon)

The white and blue of seascapes forms the basic color scheme. Leaded window-panes, neat Colonial trim, fish-net covered ceilings and recurring marine symbols (such as the lobster pattern) help create the desired atmosphere with economy and good taste

L. Souessia Photos

A BEACH CLUB TO SELL A VIEW

Ariston Restaurant, Mar del Plata, Argentina

Marcel Breuer, Carlos Coire and Eduardo F. Catalano, Architects

WHEN Marcel Breuer recently lectured at the University of Buenos Aires, two young Argentine architects, who had been instrumental in getting him invited to the University, asked him to associate on the design of a small drink-and-dance club to be constructed at the bathing resort of Mar del Plata for the purpose, primarily, of promoting the sale of plots in a nearby real estate development. This club was to be a small social center for that development — but for a start it was intended to serve as a kind of advertising booth as well, sufficiently attractive to bring in potential land buyers.

Located a little way inland from the bathing beach. the club was constructed in a setting of undulating dunes, just high enough to block the view of the ocean, unless one's eye-level were raised. Hence the stilts. The plan shows all of Mr. Breuer's clarity of organization and his painter-like appreciation of texture and form. Linked by a long field-stone wall, the two separate wings of the building contain, respectively, the staff

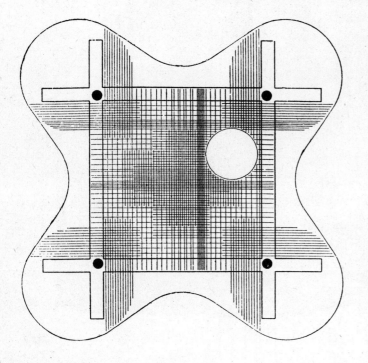

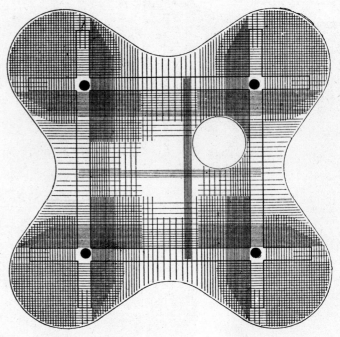

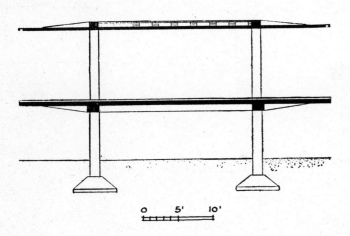

0 5' 10'

quarters and the club proper. The latter is entered on the ground level through a lobby which serves as a display and advertising area for the real estate development. An elegant spiral stair leads from this lobby to the clubroom above. Since the restaurant serves only refreshments, a small counter-type bar in one corner is all that is required.

The four-pronged plan permits each table to have window-location, and gives each window seat an arc of vision of almost 180 degrees. The playful, free-shaped clubroom is sandwiched between two two-way r.c. slabs, the roof slab having been reversed (with the girders projecting at the *top*) to produce a flat, uninterrupted ceiling surface inside. Since snow-loads need not be considered in Argentina, the roof slab can be thinner than U.S. building codes would permit. In addition, workmanship is good and inexpensive, which means that factors of safety need not be too high. The concrete employed contains basalt and mica aggregates that give it a gray, granite-like quality. The exposed underside of the ceiling slab has been given a hand-chiselled pattern, but was left otherwise unfinished. The rectangular dance floor has a parquet surface; the rest of the floor is of red tile.

The small-scale window pattern is indicative of the high cost of glass in Argentina. The exterior walls — which carry no weight and were, therefore, treated as separate entities — consist of simple stud frame partitions covered with narrow, vertical t. & g. siding. Window frames are also of wood. At certain intervals louver-type vents alternate with the window sash. With a healthy breeze from the ocean only a few hundred feet away, this is all the ventilation that is needed.

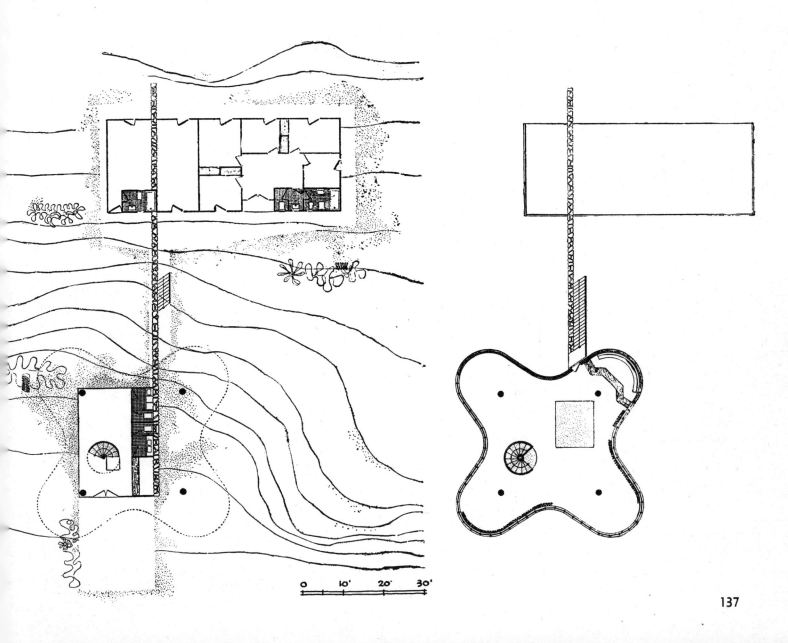

0   10'   20'   30'

TWO RESTAURANTS IN ONE

Gwinn's Restaurant, Pasadena, Calif.

Harold J. Bissner, Architect

Harold B. Zook, Architect

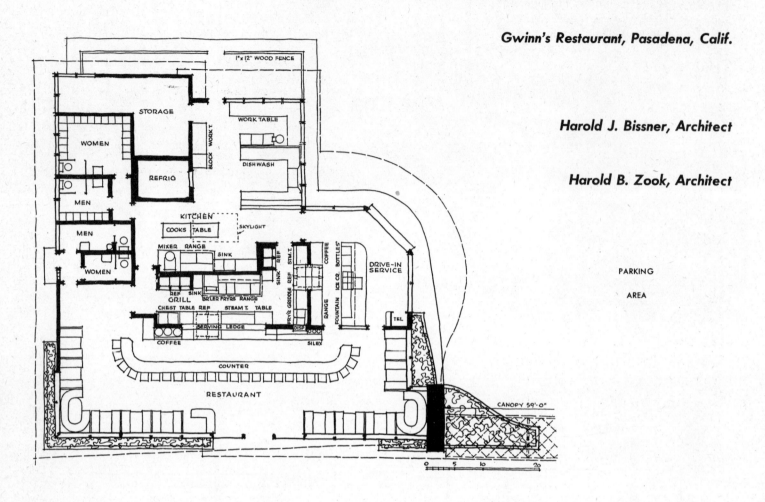

Some of the special requirements discussed with reference to Welch's Restaurant (p. 174) apply to this case as well. But in addition to providing an attractive, attention-getting design, Gwinn's architects have succeeded in creating a dual-function restaurant: one part of it is a drive-in, the other a conventional eating place.

THE PLAN of the kitchen shows excellent organization. Its various areas are carefully segregated and yet related in a very apparent flow-pattern. Food storage, food cleaning and refrigeration are grouped around the service entrance. The dishwashing area is located within easy access from either the drive-in or the restaurant proper. Food preparation is carried on centrally, so that both the restaurant counter and the drive-in counter can be supplied. And the ample employee facilities show understanding of the importance of a good staff.

To architects and laymen alike the success of the exterior treatment of Gwinn's will be obvious. The horizontal *motif* of overlapping roof planes, the finely detailed expanse of glass, and the restrained but effective "billboard" all produce in this restaurant an admirably high standard.

Julius Shulman Photos

The drive-in service opens out to the rear of the building, where there are also ample parking facilities. A small soda-fountain type of counter is used to cater especially to drive-in patrons. A weakness of the plan seems to lie in the unnecessarily complicated access from the parking lot to the main restaurant

Julius Shulman Photos

The egg-crate pattern of the free-standing canopy — obviously a device dear to the architects' hearts — extends clear back into the main restaurant. Its chief function seems to be to create a decorative accent, and as such it may, or may not, appeal to the onlooker. A further questionable detail is the alignment of the Roman brick, which, like the canopy, primarily contributes a decorative feature. Food preparation center (left) shows only a small portion of the elaborate kitchen

It is a little disappointing to find, behind so elegant and successful an exterior, an interior treatment that shows a lack of sensitive detailing. However, since most restaurant equipment is standard (and not always of the best design), the expense incurred in designing special fixtures might not be justified by the economics of restaurant operation

July 1948

GOLF CLUB RESTAURANT BRAVES SUN FOR VIEW

Cedarcrest Restaurant, Marysville, Washington

Charles R. Pearson

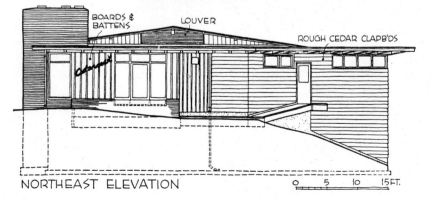

NORTHEAST ELEVATION

Harold W. Hall, Architect

Arthur A. Graves
David W. Dykeman, Jr.
Associate Architects

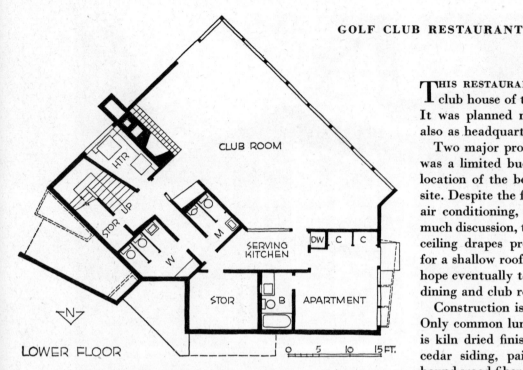

LOWER FLOOR

CLUB ROOM

HTR

STOR UP

STOR

W

M

SERVING KITCHEN

STOR

B

APARTMENT

DW C C

N

0 5 10 15 FT.

GOLF CLUB RESTAURANT

This restaurant building is situated close to the club house of the Cedarcrest (municipal) Golf Club. It was planned not only as a public restaurant, but also as headquarters for group "field days."

Two major problems complicated the planning. One was a limited budget. The other was the unfortunate location of the best view at the southwest end of the site. Despite the fact that the budget would not permit air conditioning, the entire southwest side was, after much discussion, thrown open to the view, with floor-to-ceiling drapes providing the only sun control except for a shallow roof overhang. The owners and architects hope eventually to install mechanical ventilation in the dining and club rooms.

Construction is wood frame on concrete foundation. Only common lumber was used except for trim, which is kiln dried finish material. Exterior walls are rough cedar siding, painted. Club room ceiling is cement bound wood fiber board which acts as a two-way sound barrier between the club and dining rooms.

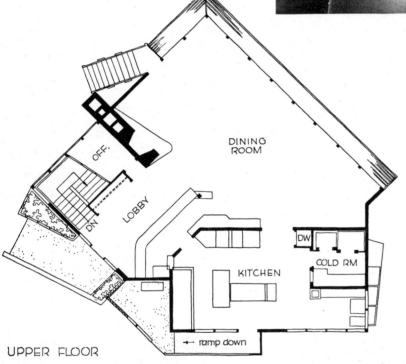

DINING
ROOM

OFF.

LOBBY

DN

DW

COLD RM

KITCHEN

← ramp down

UPPER FLOOR

Budget limitations forced compromises such as use of fir planking for dining room floor; owners hope to lay either cork or carpet in near future to help cut down noise transfer from this area to club room below. Building, complete with fixture work, cost $32,000, or slightly over $8 a square foot

Charles R. Pearson

INFORMALITY KEYNOTES RESTAURANT C

PHOENIX OUTSKIRTS

KoKo Restaurant, Phoenix, Arizona
Ralph Haver, Architect

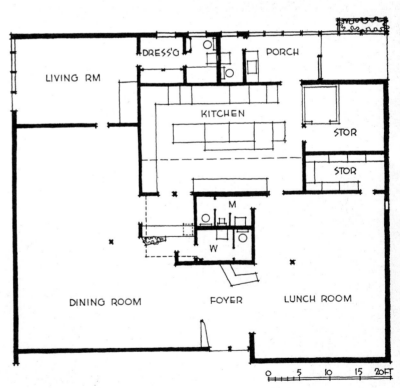

Simple rectangular plan, grouping of utilities and choice of materials not only kept costs low but also helped to achieve informal atmosphere

THE SITE SELECTED for this small restaurant is on the northern edge of Phoenix, adjacent to the winter resort area. Since prospective patrons would therefore include vacationers as well as local residents, an informal atmosphere was an obvious must. Falling in nicely with this requirement was a limited budget coupled with a limit (self-imposed) on critical materials.

Both exterior and interior are in keeping with the informal ranch-type construction typical of the area. The building is an economical rectangle, with all utilities banked for further economy. Foundation is concrete, exterior walls are pumice block; interior walls are painted pumice block or random-width boards and battens. Ceilings in the two dining areas and the owners' apartment are rough wood beams with painted fiber insulation board between the beams.

Stuart Weiner

Below: at rear of restaurant is small one-room apartment for owners. Tiny kitchen (bottom of page) is built into one end of living room

Murals add a gay note to both lunchroom-bar (left, above) and main dining room (above). Ceilings in both rooms are fiber insulation board between wood beams; lighting fixtures were architect-designed

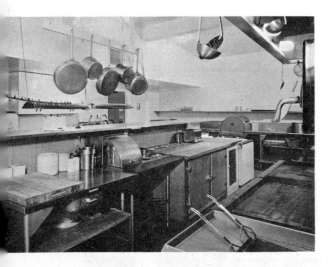

Compact restaurant kitchen (above) serves both dining areas. Ceiling here is plastered, without wood beams

EFFICIENTLY PLANNED FOR SOCIABILITY

Downtown Club, Dallas, Texas   *George Foster Harrell, Architect*

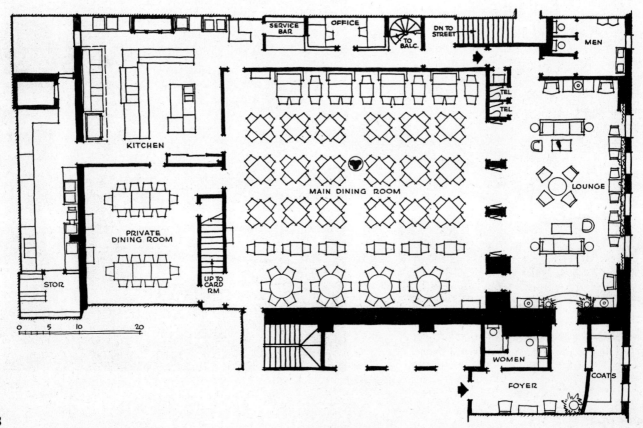

The Foyer (right) is entered from the Texas Bank Building. Direct access from the street is handled as of secondary importance. The Lounge (below) is cove-lighted

THE DOWNTOWN CLUB of Dallas adjoins the tall Texas Bank Building, from whose second floor lobby it can be entered. Designed as a private luncheon club, it was given a quiet, restful atmosphere through designer-control of such incidental details as the silverware and the china, as well as of the plan and the complete interior.

The central feature of the Downtown Club is its two-story Main Dining Room (opposite) with the five-pointed Texas star implacably in the ceiling. Grouped around the Main Dining Room are a Lounge, Private Dining Room, Card Room (on the mezzanine level) and the kitchen and work areas. The latter, especially, show careful attention to efficient planning. Staff facilities are on the mezzanine also, with spiral stair.

The Private Dining Room (right) can be sub-divided by a folding screen into two smaller areas for more intimate parties. It is within easy reach of the kitchen area. Note the air conditioning grilles at the ceiling — part of the year-round system designed for this Club

RESTAURANTS AND BARS

Ben Schnall Photos

ARCHITECTURE FOR EATING AND DRINKING

By Herman H. Siegel

RESTAURANT: "An establishment where refreshments or meals may be procured by the public; a public eating house" — Webster. Actually it is a generic term embracing all kinds and manifestations of "public eating house." However, the word may also convey the special sense of a more or less elaborate type, where the service is predominantly by waiter or waitress.

At points where fashion and luxury become clearly subordinate to the customer's budget of time and money, we shall make further type differentiations as: Cafeteria, or predominantly self-service type restaurant; Luncheonette, or predominantly counter type restaurant. There are also such sub-types as: Drive-in, or roadside restaurants (see ARCHITECTURAL RECORD, Sept. '46, pp. 99–106, for detailed treatment); Oyster Bars, Ham 'n' Eggeries, Hamburger Heavens, and other similar forms of speciality service.

These sub-types, aside from their special functional requirements, involved chiefly the same planning and design considerations to be treated here under the primary classifications. Such pseudo types as "Tea Rooms," "Rathskellars," etc. differ mostly according to "atmosphere," and not essential function.

BARS, whether independent services or integral features in all the foregoing restaurant types, vary chiefly in degree rather than kind, and are treated in a comprehensive section.

LIGHTING and KITCHENS, foremost factors for commercial (and esthetic) success in all types, are given separate analysis.

Photos left, right: Sakele's, Brooklyn. Top: Tropical Gardens, N. Y. City. Herman Siegel, Architect; Ernest D. Rapp, Designer. S. Y. Construction Co. were general contractors for Sakele's

THE definition of *Restaurant* might really be extended to bring it under the broader concept of *Store*. For after all, restaurants of every type and sub-type are strictly in the business of merchandising food. The same fundamentals of planning and design are involved here as in any other selling operation — first, analyzing and organizing factors of receipt, storage, processing and delivery of the goods for sale, in this case cookery and drink items; then, the attraction, distribution, comfort and convenience of customers.

It seems to me, from the point of comparative advantage in experience with both, that the principal difference for the architect, between restaurants and stores in the more usual sense, is that there are more

This globe, one of three in Sakeles' main dining room, gives general light, relieves a disproportionately high ceiling, and transmits ineluctable attraction to the glimpser from street

inherent complications in the former. Foremost among these are architectural-engineering problems in the nature of the factory production line. This crucial element of food "manufactury," in planning kitchens in relationship to other restaurant areas, is discussed at length on pages 180 to 182.

The Restaurant General Plan. Every restaurant operation is of course unique, even among chains, in that it follows to some extent its own methods and notions in catering to a predominant client type, existing for a particular location. However, it may be said that *all* restaurants are subject to a general plan, almost always involving consideration of the following basic elements: *entrance areas*, *dining areas*, *kitchen areas*, and frequently *bars* and cocktail lounges.

Entrance Areas: *Exteriors, Entrances and Anterooms.* In all restaurant types — down to the most frenetic luncheonette — exterior appearance, as a first consideration, should imply the particular operation's essential character. Within this figurative limitation, elements of the exterior must then *attract*, *advertise*, and *compel* to the entrance, and then inside, the patronage desired. Further, and within *material* limitations, the exterior treatment must take in account the contingent nature of existing locations (a condition imposed on the architect in perhaps 75 per cent of cases). The restaurant

front should be distinctive, *not* disharmonious, in its given surroundings.

As a possible example, I shall cite Sakeles' (see photos pp. 150-151), where effort was made to achieve definite character and compulsiveness in the front, at the same time regarding it as a compositional element in a larger given setting. To an existing fascia of cast stone and glass brick, the marble pier was added as architectural background for vertical signs advertising name and function. Within a new plaster surround, large glass areas with stainless steel trim were put at glare-reductive angles.

From this example, I believe it is possible to illustrate another cardinal tenet in treating the front. Restaurant windows should expose, where possible, to potential patronage outside, all manners and varieties of inducement to come and dine within. Among these is the spectacle of diners already on location, enjoying appetizing food amid conducive surroundings and brisk service. Perhaps this exposé technique is less applicable to restaurants (in the restrictive sense) of the larger and more fashionable type; certainly, it is less so in cases such as Sakeles', catering not so much to a transient trade which must be induced, as to a more or less repetitive clientele. Sakeles', however, will serve to illustrate the point. Note in the photographs that behind the windows of the right-hand (dining-area) half, the curtains are partially open, to disclose not only a suggestive view of the diners and services within but also of such compulsive internal features, projecting their attractions through to the outside, as the globe of light illustrated on this page. Note also that the curtains on the left-hand, or bar-area, side are tightly drawn, permitting no certain disclosures either of internal features or of imbibing patrons (about which nicety more will be said later). Field's Restaurant, illustrated on this page, shows these principles carried architecturally further.

Exterior treatment should reflect restaurant *character*, as we have shown, and as character varies further according to *type*, from the large restaurant with its

Field's, New York City. Large restaurant window (left) discloses features within; discreet bar window (right) discloses mostly bottles. Separate bar entrance, far right. (Siegel – Rapp)

Ben Schnall Photos

air of veiled dignity — perhaps even seclusiveness — through the lesser *chi-chi* varieties, down to the cafeteria and luncheonette, we find the tendency in fronts toward more and more openness and forthright disclosure of what goes on inside. *Chockfull o' Nuts* is a widespread example of a luncheonette chain disclosing its *all* to street visibility. (See also page 170.) The completely open front of Reed's, a cafeteria illustrated on this page, is intended to show off the food-selection counter to outside appraisal, as a major inducement to enter in and partake.

The technique of bringing the actual service and even preparation of food out as far as possible through the show window is by no means confined to self-service and counter types. *Lindy's* and the *Brass Rail*, famous big operations in New York City, have contributed to the fad of refrigerated show windows, in which the displays of meat, fish, and fowl and vegetable vary according to season. Other forms of such display are the featuring of liquor, where the cellar is celebrated, or pastries, where baking is a house specialty. And then there are all the processes of hamburger, griddle-cake and do-nut making shown directly in the front window. Every one of the "glorifried" ham 'n' eggs served to patrons in the specialty sub-type houses of that name, are prepared in full view of the potential customer looking on from the sidewalk.

Entrances, the actual doors, obviously should be the operative climax of all the attractive and compulsive efforts put into the exterior as a whole — a flawlessly operating springboard to the inside. Architects generally, I should assume, are already enough aware of the many marketed possibilities in full or semi-glass doors, operating on gravity hinges, etc., and responding like gelatin to push or pull, that I need not enlarge on this point. However, I should like to emphasize that wherever possible, in my own practice, I plan separate outside entrances into bar and restaurant areas under one roof, as in Sakeles' and Field's.

Anterooms. These areas will be strictly defined, of course, only in the larger operations, perhaps as foyers, vestibules, lounges, etc. In the less elaborate restaurant types, they tend to become simply open space allowances for circulation and orientation of entering and departing traffic; and in these respects must be carefully calculated, according to seating capacity and internal circulation, to avoid conflicts detrimental to trade.

Checkrooms and cashier-counter fixtures in these spaces should be unmistakably evident, but, if possible, not *obtrusive*. Wash and retiring rooms for customers are sometimes provided in anteroom areas. Preferably these facilities should be as close as possible to dining room and bar, certainly on the same level at least, although in many cases they are tucked up or down stairs to conserve essential service or dining space. This is an equilibrium that every architect must work out for himself in each particular situation.

The design of Reed's Cafeteria, New York City, is intended to give theatrical starring to its biggest selling feature, the counter, with large areas of glass on both street sides making complete disclosure of the interior. Self-service and counter-type operations make a particular practice of this, as if to emphasize, with all their business and bustle, that no dirt can ever gather in hidden pockets and corners, as the observer from outside can readily see for himself.

In the section above, note use of acoustical material, especially functional in self-service operations where customers handle trays with less finesse than professional bearers. Counter back-wall is of tile for cleanliness. Fresh air, circulated from outlets indicated, returns to exhaust ducts over service counter (see sketch page 182). Marble slab adds front distinctiveness; demarks bar and dining areas (see plan page 160). Floors will be green and white terrazzo. Photo below shows progress as of June 6. Siegel, Architect; Rapp, Designer; Chase Construction Co., General Contractors. Sketches by Ernest D. Rapp.

Alfred Cook Photo

Alfred Cook Photos

area capacity, and to circulation allowances for customers and service between the seat and table combinations finally adopted. When, within these limitations, a workable numerical maximum has been calculated, the architect must then persuade the owner to let him make it really effective with variations and combinations among Continental settees, Hollywood settees, Pullman booths, and ordinary tables and chairs, whether stock or custom built. *Seating variations* cannot be over-emphasized and the most fortunate architect in this respect is the one whose site and given circumstances permit him to vary his dining-room floor levels, enabling patrons to look up or down at their public eating companions. (For example, see project illustrated on page across.) Such variations in level are useful also in planning to make dining areas expansible or contractible in keeping with fluctuations of custom.

Dining-Area Equipment and Materials. Seating: the very best booths and settees, I believe, are those constructed of hardwood frames, coil-spring seats topped with "air-foam" cushions, and spring backs with "air-foam" pads. A popular and serviceable covering is leatherette. Numerous plastics are now being used as covering material, but I believe they should be regarded largely as still experimental. Mohair fabric is sometimes used, but it is not nearly so wear-resistant nor easily cleaned.

Left: Glorifried Ham 'n' Eggs, N. Y. City; Samar Construction Co., Dsnrs. Below: Hollywood settees in Sakeles'; Continental settees, Pullman booths, along left wall; Rubber tile floor

Entrance-Area Materials and Equipment. A salutary trend here, I believe, is away from such veneers as porcelain enamel, and even architectural glass, toward more use of brick, terra cotta, cast stone, terrazzo and marble, the suitability and proportions of each in any application to be determined by existing building relationships and the intent and character of the particular operation. Where the novelty technique in exterior expression involves refrigeration — as in Gallagher's Steak House, with the raw primary product displayed in the front window — consideration must be given to impervious show-case linings such as tile, Carrara glass or marble. And, of course, the surrounding clear glass areas must be triple-glazed, or otherwise adequately insulative.

In designing windows for liquor display, remember that these items are highly subject to pilfer, and must be safeguarded in some form of secure enclosure.

Dining Areas. Here the architect frequently finds himself using his persuasive utmost to bring the owner down from dreams of numerical seating maxima to realistic figuring on the number and types of seats most *effective* for his kind of business. I believe that in any kind of operation (excluding the strictly counter-seat), so-called "Pullman booths," used entirely, will accommodate more customers than any other seating method. This solution, on the other hand, is obviously static and uninteresting and does not, in my opinion, provide an *effective* long-range maximum. Furthermore, the architect, in working with the owner on the seating question, must continually be thinking of relationships to kitchen-

Ben Schnall Photos

Left: plastic-top, chrome-pedestal table in Hollywood booth at Tropical Gardens. Curtain is glass fabric; floor, asphalt tile; color scheme, red, white and mahogany. Above: table tops in Field's are plastic "real wood." Certain table units here (not those in center, see left and right) illustrate the principle of "deuces," that is basic two-placers that can be almost endlessly combined, but do not permit space wastage by one or two patrons. Floor is asphalt tile; walls are mahogany wainscot. Below: restaurant project for Florida. Siegel, Architect; Rapp, Designer. Seating is on rising levels not only for variety and flexibility, but also for picture-window view. Arrangement for air conditioning outlet and intake system (see section) is considered close to ideal. Special sketches by Ernest D. Rapp

Settee and booth seats should be at least 18 in. deep and about 18 in. high. Standard booth width for one person is 26 in.; for two, 44 in. Back heights seldom should exceed 4 ft.

Chairs are preferably constructed of hardwood frames, with innerspring units covered by a layer of hair and at least 2 in. of "air-foam," then muslin and top covering. Backs and arms of chairs should be separated from seats to prevent débris collecting. Booth seats and backs, for like reason, should be removable.

Tables. Primary considerations here, as with other furniture, should be wear resistance and ease of maintenance. Hardwood tops are fine looking, particularly in "atmosphere" operations, but are greatly subject to stain and cigarette burns and require ceaseless attention. Thickness of hardwood tops should be between $7/8$ and $1\frac{1}{8}$ in. In restaurants making full use of table cloths, unfinished plywood tops are a possibility.

Probably for all-around utility, linoleum or plastic tops are the best specification, with the latter being particularly impervious to wear and easily maintained. The architect, however, should be certain of what's beneath the surface. Best foundations for both linoleum and plastic are $7/8$ to $1\frac{1}{8}$-in. plywood panels, with the top layer hardwood to prevent ripples in the surface covering. Lumber should be kiln-dried and the glue waterproof. Edging should be stainless steel.

Chrome-plated pipe *pedestals*, of about 4-in. diameter, are quite satisfactory. Four-legged tables are no longer much in evidence, because of the irksomeness of cleaning around them. *Bases* are preferably one solid piece, the

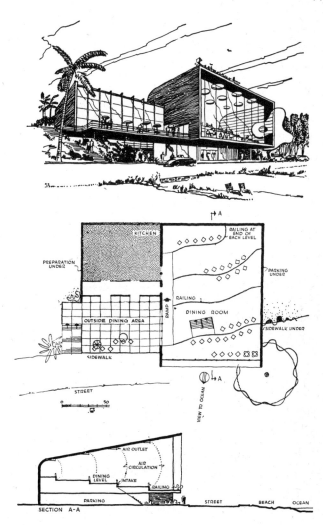

Ben Schnall Photos

heavier and broader, the more stable and desirable. Tables on *carpet* should have *heavy bases with broad spread*.

Floor coverings may be considered under two general headings: *resilient*, including asphalt tile (plain and greaseproof), plastic tiles, linoleum and linoleum tile, rubber tile, cork and carpet; *rigid*, including glazed tile, quarry tile, magnesium composition, colored concrete, terrazzo and slate. Bases for the resilient types must be smooth and even (nail heads and grains of sand will show up under rubber tile, blemishing the wax finish; uneven flooring will cause cracks in asphalt tile). A well-laid double wood floor is usually successful with resilient types; also, *smooth* concrete.

Asphalt tile gives long wear for low cost, and is much less subject to chair and table-leg indentation than linoleum. Obviously the greaseproof variety is preferable for restaurant use. It is available in a wide range of colors in three grades, of which "Deluxe" affords the best selection. Easiest obtainable sizes, currently, are 9 by 9-in. squares, and 9 by 4-in. strips for borders and divisions. Thickness of $3/16$ in. is recommended for wood bases; $1/8$ in., for concrete.

Plastic tiles give long grease-, acid-, and practically waterproof wear in a wide variety of colors, but are at present still hard to get in quantity. The resin types, in my experience, give best performance.

Linoleum is again available in many colors and patterns, and with burlap backing, the only type to be considered for restaurant use. It tends to disintegrate under standing water and excessive heat; in these respects the "lino tiles" (oil-bonded finish) are a major improvement.

Rubber tile, in my opinion, is the best looking and among the best wearing of all the resilient types. It is also a great aid in acoustical treatment.

Carpet, of course, is the richest appearing and most resiliently luxurious of all coverings, and the most expensive. In general, I might say that both wool and worsted *Wiltons* are preferable to *Velvets* and *Axminsters* where heavy traffic is expected. *Chenille* weaves are woven seamless up to 30 ft., in width, have great sturdiness, luxuriousness, and variety in color and design.

Quarry tile, among the rigid floorings, is practically a *must* for Tavern "atmosphere." It is extremely durable and easily cleaned.

Terrazzo is probably the most durable and effortlessly maintained of all materials, withstanding wear almost like solid marble. In addition, the marble chips can be "composed" in patterns and color effects. Size of the pattern squares is important; the smaller they are with more division strips, the better chance of contraction and expansion without cracking.

Almost all the foregoing flooring types are benefitted by faithful waxing, which seals the surface and helps maintain the original colors.

Wall-Finish materials to substantial degree may be considered as extensions of floor coverings, since many of these, like terrazzo and the various tiles, natural and synthetic, are used effectively in such application, particularly in self-service and counter operations. Also varieties of the table-top plastics are available, in special wall color patterns and "realwood" textures, for counter fronts and wainscoting. All of these materials can

Top: ceiling in Field's is of stone-type acoustical tile, fissured surface; draperies are by Dan Cooper; Adler Construction Co., General Contractors. Below: decorations and murals in

Tropical Gardens were designed by Winold Reiss, executed by Imperial Painting Co.; Karl Egger was the General Contractor. Note in photo, right, the "deuce" principle in Continental settee

"take it" and are easily maintained, absolutely indispensable qualities along with "attractiveness" in restaurant specification.

For the fancier operations, hardwood ply paneling, varnished or lacquered, still rates high in withstanding time and abuse, though requiring frequent refinishing. This material, where curved surfaces are a factor, can be very costly and, in this respect, the flexible veneers on canvas or metal effect great saving. A newcomer among these (on metal) has the further advantage of flexibility without wood filler.

Acoustical materials are conditioned by legal restrictions in certain metropolitan areas; for example, in Class I buildings, fire-resistant materials must be used throughout; in Class III, 50 per cent of materials may be combustible, but not to exceed 3000 sq. ft.

Acoustical tile of the stone type comes in both plain and fissured surfaces. Paint (other than water-base) causes appreciable loss in sound-absorbing efficiency.

Perforated acoustical tile comes in both fire-resistant and combustible forms, in two thicknesses for varying conditions; can be painted repeatedly.

Perforated cement asbestos board with "rock-wool" or glass-fiber filler pads also can be painted.

Offending restaurant noises center at a frequency of about 512; any material selected should have a high sound-absorbing coefficient at this cyclic rate.

Air Conditioning, as a dining-area factor, is discussed under this heading in the kitchen planning section.

Above: front door of Tropical Gardens illustrates the principle in bar design of compulsive expression on the exterior, proclaiming but not disclosing the functions within. Below, left: bar in Field's is set apart from dining area by dropped ceiling and open fin-and-fluted-glass partition; dome lighting is cold-cathode

BARS

FORTHRIGHT disclosure in this department is definitely *not* in keeping, even where the service is offered in connection with a self-service restaurant such as Reed's (see page 153 and plan, page 160). Although prominent citizens may properly assert they "have nothing to hide" in occasional temperate indulgence, still they don't really like to do it on manifest exhibition. For this reason the exterior of Tropical Gardens (see page 151, as well as photo above), though striving for attractiveness and compulsion in line with principles for the restaurant front, has much smaller window areas, with curtains as a rule nearly drawn, to reveal very little to the street of the activities and personages inside. Still the front should express, as Tropical Gardens attempts, particularly in the doorway, the essential nature and character of the

Sakele's bar front and stools are covered in a red plastic material, padded. Bar top, display frames and paneling are of Mexican mahogany. Ceiling is Burgundy; walls are a deep red, to give warmth and intimacy in an unusually spacious bar area. Above far end of the bar, note balustrade of mezzanine dining space

Ben Schnall Photos

Below: checkered bar front in Solly Krieger's, New York City, is padded maroon and beige leatherette; top is Mexican mahogany. Step in lieu of usual bar foot-rest gives variety

In both Solly Krieger's and Field's Bar (below), glassware and bottles are given emphatic play as essentially decorative bar-area elements, with bullet-type spotlights focussing directly on them. Field's bar front provides a variation in use of striped mahogany plywood; top is a solid slab of Mexican mahogany. Dropped ceiling, which not only gives bar intimacy but conceals conduit and air conditioning ducts, is of stone-type acoustical tile with a fissured surface

operation, projecting all possible inducements to make the customer enter.

Field's Bar (photos on page preceding and left, below) shows how this area may be sequestered, to give it the required air of intimacy and privacy, from the dining areas, at the same time maintaining all possible feeling of spaciousness in fairly close overall quarters. Sakele's Bar (photos, left), a genuinely spacious area, is separated from the main dining room (see pages 152 and 154) by an existing structural wall. Still, in this large space with a high ceiling, the essential feeling of intimacy is sought through use of warm dark colors and subdued lighting.

Ceiling height was also a problem in Tropical Gardens (right), this being a full 16 ft., with walls only 20 ft. apart. The bar canopy, in conjunction with cove lighting over Winold Reiss's mural on the wall opposite, most economically reduces this ungainly dimension to an apparent 10 ft., with everything above almost completely blacked out. Moreover, this device effectively sets off the bar area from the dining regions, with food here a subordinate service to liquor.

Tropical Gardens bar front, directly above, is red leatherette with mahogany top. The same materials were used on the bar of Lottie's Dogwood Room (below, left), New York City, where the problem was to provide an intimate new bar in an existing room with a set "atmosphere." This was accomplished by a suspended ceiling and special lighting fixtures in the domes, similar to "pin points," for low intensity. Photo top, left, is of service bar at Cafe Wienicke, New York City; patterns are linoleum cutouts on plywood. Below is the Wienicke patron's bar. Siegel, Architect; Rapp, Designer, for all jobs on these two pages

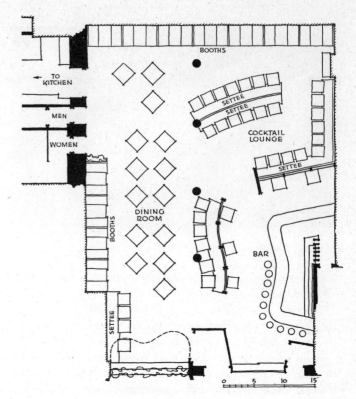

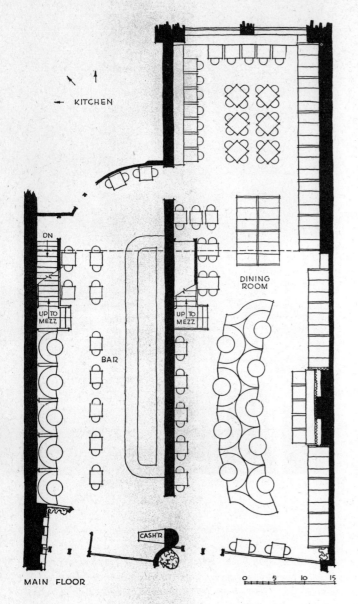

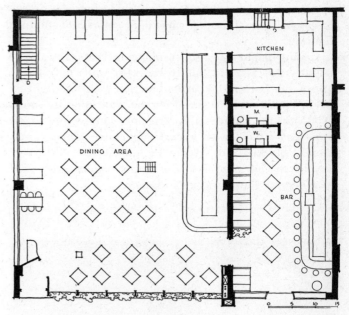

KITCHEN

DINING ROOM

ON

UP TO MEZZ

UP TO MEZZ

BAR

DINING ROOM

CASH'R

MAIN FLOOR

Plan of Sakele's, directly above, shows bar and dining areas demarked by existing wall. Dotted line indicates mezzanine with two dining areas especially adapted for private parties. Rear portion of main dining room can be screened off during lulls. Bar and dining areas in Field's, upper right, though more closely associated, are still distinct. Plan of Reed's Cafeteria, right, depends largely on relationship of counter to kitchen

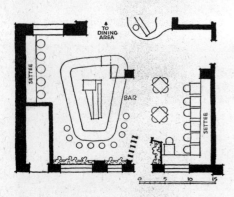

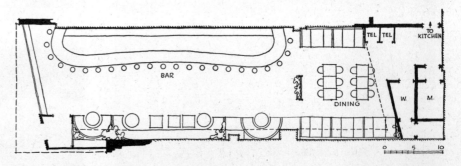

Left: awkward arrangement of existing columns had to be overcome in providing intimate bar with hung ceiling for Lottie's Dogwood Room. Above: plan of Tropical Gardens

Moulin Studios Photos

NEW "OUT-OF-DOORS" CAFE OYSTER AND LIQUOR BARS

Grison's Steak House, San Francisco

Hertzka & Knowles, Architects

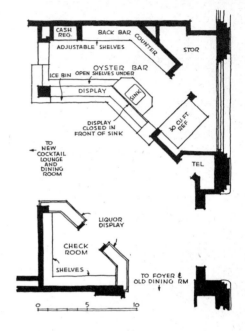

TAKING space from two adjoining shops on Pacific Avenue, the architects have added, to the facilities of this renowned steak-and-chop house, new sea food and liquor bars, a cocktail lounge, and dining room giving the illusion of an out-of-doors café, with its vine-covered trellis and murals suggestive of Palm Springs. The problem was "to provide attractions for new customers, without frightening away or offending old trade."

Walls are knotty pine, stained dark; covering suggest-ing brick was designed by Van Luit. Ceiling is knotty pine and acoustical board, painted blue. Display case of oyster bar is copper and glass, with blue background wall on which are mounted crab and oyster shells gathered from local beaches. Top of cocktail bar is Scotch wool-plaid, made impervious to burns and stains with plastic impregnation; trim is copper. W. Adrian was Engineer; Elizabeth Banning, was the Color Consultant.

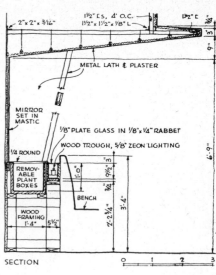

SECTION

Hedrich-Blessing Photos

NEW HORIZON ROOM
CONTINENTAL HOTEL

Chicago, Ill.

Holabird & Root, Architects

IN providing new horizons for this bar and restaurant, the architects have carried the mirror technique to points of unusual refinement. In the main dining area (photo at top), primordial creatures are depicted directly on the glass, set into a mural of their natural habitat under a broad overhang of plaster canopy. The motif is echoed in the bar, where the canopy has less formality, and jungle vegetation flanks a mirror left clear to receive the images of stool-top patrons. A three-step descent reaches the interconnecting dining area.

Front of bar is a field of padded black patent leather, against which are set 2-in. yellow-leather buttons. Bar top and back-bar working surfaces are plastic. Base is black and white terrazzo with brass dividers.

BAR AND RESTAURANT
FOR HOTEL MCALPIN

New York City

Kahn and Jacobs, Architects

Planned and carried out as part of the major overhauling given to the McAlpin's entire first floor — to receive the Crawford Clothing chain's new headquarters store (see pp. 90-95, July '47 issue)—this bar and restaurant has given immense lift to the hotel business. Major feature is a 90-ft. serpentine bar, with a front of wood intarsia by Hildreth Meiere. Back-bar murals of glass-and-marble mosaic, representing the nation's four principal geographical regions, are also by Meiere. Michael L. Radoslovich, architect in the office of Kahn and Jacobs, coordinated all the McAlpin renovations.

Bar entrance is off 34th Street; marquee at top of photograph is that of Hotel's main entrance. In photo below, ceiling cove lighting is cold-cathode; bar cove has regular fluorescent tubes

Ben Schnall Photos

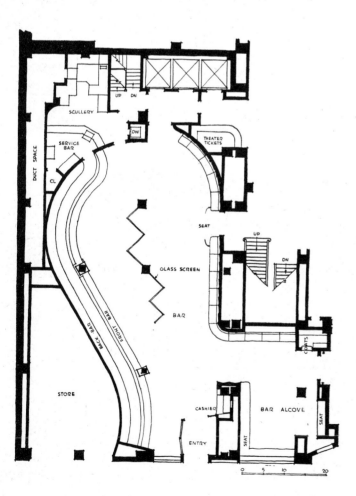

Ben Schnall Photos

Paneling in bar alcove (left) and main area (below, left) is flexible plywood on metal, mahogany finish. Floor is black and white terrazzo with stainless-steel dividers. Entrance off hotel lobby (below, right) is faced with Colorado Colorosa marble

MADISON ROOM

FOR DAY AND EVENING SERVICE IN A DEPARTMENT STORE

H. S. Manchester, Inc., Madison, Wis.

Skidmore, Owings & Merrill, Architects

THIS double operation is unusual for a department store — by day serving store customers, for the most part, and in the evening, general outside patronage. Opening at 10:00 every morning and closing at 9:00 p.m., it offers four basic services: luncheon, afternoon tea, pre-

Smith-Wollin Photos

Photos left and below show views of State Capitol and grounds afforded by the Manchester Madison Room, ''unequalled by any other restaurant on Capitol Square, and particularly impressive at night.'' Draperies are by Angelo Testa; furniture is natural-finish birch; light-brown grospoint carpet covers dining area. View above shows street-entrance vestibule, with checkroom, left, and settees for waiting patrons. Note ''Running Men'' wallpaper at right; background wall is deep brown

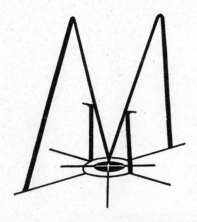

Symbol, left, designed by Rainey Bennett, appears on the menu covers, china, flatware, place mats, match-folders, Petri-dish ash trays, and as a free-standing wall fixture against the "Running Men" background (see top photo, page across). The two "M's", on compass axis, suggest Madison as the hub of the state, and Manchester's, near to the Capitol, as the center of the city

Smith-Wollin Photos

theater suppers, and full dinners. It is one of the first phases to reach completion in Manchester's considerable building-and-alterations program.

Located on the second floor of the store's new addition, the restaurant has one entrance directly from selling areas, and another by stairs from the street. During shopping hours, only the store entrance is open, to draw traffic through the selling departments; in the evening, access is from the street alone. The consequence is a daytime patronage predominantly of women, with a much greater representation of men at night, requiring the general design to have appeal in both directions, with avoidance of an atmosphere too

"tea-roomy." Another design requirement was that decor be keyed to Madison's out-of-door and sports way of living.

In this spirit, the stairwell slab wall is covered with "Running Men" wall paper, a Danish import designed by Kirby; the same motif appears on the menu covers, by Chicago artist Rainey Bennett (see top page 166). The slab wall of natural-finish white ash, before the kitchen entrance, features depiction of a major regional sport, and in the street-entrance vestibule, casein paintings, also by Mr. Bennett, show scenes around Madison: the lake, State Capitol building, and other features of historical and sporting interest.

Photos on this page show stair entrance from street, right, and entrance from department store selling areas, below, with folding screen closed for night operation. Table lamps (right, see also page 166) were designed and executed by Isamu Noguchi; gooseneck fixtures (below) by Kurt Versen. Store-entrance and kitchen walls are gray; ceilings, oyster-white acoustical plaster

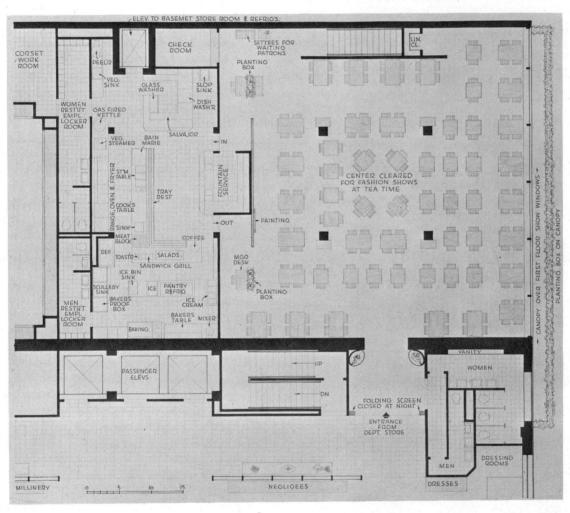

In the plan above, seating is provided for 160. Restroom facilities for men and women are convenient at store entrance; checkroom, used mostly at night, is directly opposite street entrance. The kitchen and service areas show many features certified by experts (see pages 180-182), with distinct "In" and "Out" doorways, efficient fixture layout and convenient employee facilities

Lionel Freedman: Pictorial Services Photos

RENAISSANCE AT RIKER'S

Broadway and 104th St. New York City
By Daniel Laitin, A.I.A.

THIS newest link in the Riker's chain presents almost all the unique problems usually confronting an architect with a stool-type restaurant on his boards.

In the first place, the allowed space for such operations is always about as big as a postage stamp. In a tightly limited area, the architect must somehow manage to fit most of the amenities of a large restaurant, never losing sight of the fact that cleverness and tricks of design must always be subordinate to *"Operation Food."* Dishes must be cooked and brought to the customer with dispatch, yet looking attractive. And "turnover" in this type of eatery is the key to its success or failure. This unit is in a hotel with access from the lobby.

Employee locker facilities, storage of canned goods, compressors, etc., were relegated to the cellar. Nevertheless, it took considerable juggling and slide-rule manipulation to fit all the necessary equipment into the tight space, and still come out with seats for 32 paying occupants. It has long been accepted that no waitress can serve more than 10 customers with proper efficiency, so three U-shape counters were used, with two places at the far end near the hotel entrance for bellhop service. The girls at this station call their orders on a speaker and pick them up a minute or two later on a conveyor belt, which returns soiled dishes to the washer.

The owners gave the architect complete freedom in the design, merely stipulating that he use some panels of glass mosaic, seemingly *de rigueur* for New York restaurants just now. Lately, the orgy of abortive misuse of glass mosaic, an intrinsically beautiful material and expensive, too ($7.00 a sq. ft.), has caused conscientious architects to writhe and fume. This opportunity to do something about it could not be muffed! Artist Max Spivak, a glass mosaic expert with an imagination like Miro and a sense of color precision like Stuart Davis, accepted the challenge and came up with several delightful and colorful abstracts. The architect and artist believe that here they have brought art out of the museum and onto the street to be judged forthrightly and critically by the public. The response to these frequently misunderstood spatial fantasies has been terrific. One customer marvelled at the fact that the shapes took on new character each time she came in to eat.

The vibrant colors of the abstracts are keynotes for the interior color scheme, which includes spinach green, carrot red and butter yellow. Ceramic mosaic tile on the rear wall and behind the stainless steel equipment is matt black. Cold-cathode cove lighting gives smooth primary light distribution, and bullet-type hanging reflectors supply incandescent light where necessary to give the food its proper colors for good appetite.

RESTAURANT LIGHTING WITH SLEIGHT-OF-HAND

By Thomas Smith Kelly, Chairman, N. Y. Section, I.E.S.

CURRENT implications are that the general practice of lighting tends more and more in the direction of an exactly quantitative science. Probably this is most true in cases of laboratories or libraries, where critical seeing tasks are the factors of first importance. However, in restaurants and bars, the rather unscientific factor of "atmosphere" is at least equally ponderable. Strict standards of visibility come closest to being all-important in kitchen areas, and in cafeterias and luncheonettes, where customers select food directly as "merchandise," rather than from a menu. But otherwise, restaurant lighting experts not only must be methodical technicians, but must know the techniques of theater and stage-set, and downright sleight-of-hand!

All practitioners do well, of course, to start within the framework of recommended lighting levels, such as those published by I.E.S., or by the larger manufacturers. Quoting a cross-sectional example: "for restaurants, lunchrooms, and cafeterias, it is recommended that corridors be provided with 5 f.c.; dining room areas, with 10 f.c.; kitchens, pantries and serving areas, with 20 f.c. Displays, 50 f.c."

But, first, on a particular job, the lighting expert must familiarize himself *absolutely* with every dimension, surface, material, color and other architectural specification involved in the areas to be lighted. In addition to the tool of light-source *intensity*, there is that of *color;* and in addition to both, there are many traps for the unwary in the way of their use. There are excessive brightness contrasts to be avoided between light and dark surfaces (anything over 10 to 1 is very questionable); and mirrors and other specular surfaces must be guarded to prevent reflected glare, inimical to customer mood and comfort.

Color, in this mood respect, is most important. Among the major reasons for fluorescent lighting's popularity is its efficiency of lumen output, and the most efficient of all fluorescent varieties is the so-called "daylight" lamp. But under this source alone, with its red spectrum deficiency, restaurant operators and customers find their coffee looking gray, their roast beef, anemic; and ladies' make-ups, de-glamorized.

Speaking generally, the incandescent lamp is the best source of light where food and facial complexions are concerned, since it provides the complete solar spectrum. Frequently it works well in this connection simply as a mixing element with fluorescent. For showcases, glass-faced refrigerators, etc., soft white fluorescent may be used, producing satisfactory color values, and at the same time less heat against the refrigerant than equal-wattage incandescent.

Whatever the means chosen for various uses and effects, modifications will surely be necessary in recommended area levels. For example, in a dining room where the atmosphere is to be strictly *intime*, tabular recommendations of 10 f.c. may be way out of line.

Regarding intensity calculations in general, it is usually wise, in early planning stages, to figure on *over*lighting, since intensities as a rule can more easily be reduced than increased, once a job is completed. Ultimately, of course, even in self-service operations where intimacy and relaxation are not of the first order, avoidance of *too much* light in any area is the one absolute rule to be laid down. But at the outset, lighting experts cannot really anticipate what owners will judge in the end to be the effects that *they* want, nor what refinements the architect or decorator will make in ceilings, walls, flooring, table tops, draperies, etc., adding to the final problems of light reflection and absorption.

In his overall approach to the possibilities of a particular assignment, the lighting expert will certainly prescribe nothing that does not harmoniously complement the architect's efforts and effects, nor those of the decorator. He will start with the exterior in prescribing

Lighting at far end of Sakele's main dining room is designed to supplement globes in drawing customer circulation into this area

Ben Schnall Photos

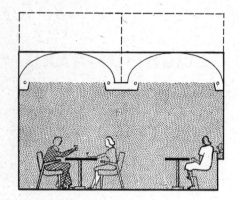
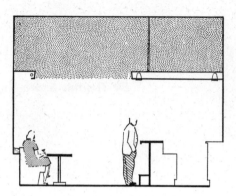

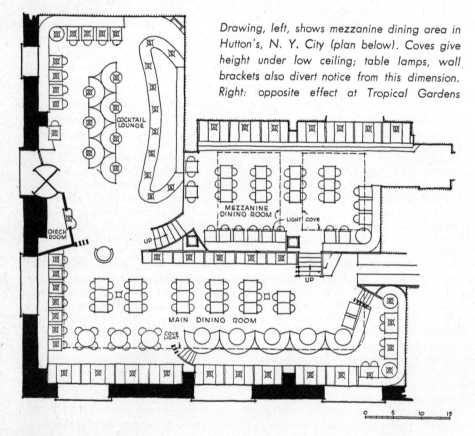

Drawing, left, shows mezzanine dining area in Hutton's, N. Y. City (plan below). Coves give height under low ceiling; table lamps, wall brackets also divert notice from this dimension. Right: opposite effect at Tropical Gardens

COCKTAIL LOUNGE

CHECK ROOM

MEZZANINE DINING ROOM

LIGHT COVE

UP

UP

MAIN DINING ROOM

COVE LIGHT

0 5 10 15

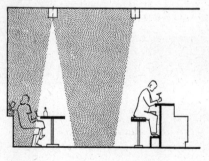

Above, left: in Hutton's bar "pin-hole" projectors, centered over table and bar tops, give areas of intimate "isolation." In main dining room, right, coves supply chief light, with two chandeliers for sparkle. Lowered area, under ducts, has "pin-hole" system. In plan, R represents pin-holes; S, surface mounted; U, indirect urns. H. H. Siegel, Architect; E. D. Rapp, Designer. Thomas Smith Kelly, Lighting Consultant

for architectural *attraction*, and for internal features of *compulsion*, possibly a chandelier or illuminated mural, magnetically visible to outside observers.

Sleight-of-hand makes its ultimate contribution in lighting for *concealment*, such as throwing displeasing but unavoidable structural features into obscurity, by accentuating attractive points of interest. An example is in Tropical Gardens (see pp. 90-95 July '47 issue) where lighting effects are instrumental in reducing a disproportionate 16-ft. ceiling to an apparent 10.

But here also, the lighting expert must be wary. The principle of architecturally built-in lighting is generally sound, but mistakes, or devices that lose their charm, are expensive to correct. Coves particularly can be disappointing. Remember that even with a matte-finish ceiling it is difficult to get from coves an advantage much greater than three to one. That is, to get a smooth spread across a 5-ft. ceiling, the coves on either side must be at least a foot down from the ceiling line (allowing for necessary overlap).

The expert who bears in mind these admonitions, and calculates all his factors with precision and imagination, still cannot be confident of his results until tested against public reaction. Lighting, like architecture itself, can be correctly executed according to every technical and artistic canon and still fall resoundingly flat before popular judgment. Close to supreme achievement, I think, is in a job recently offered to a prominent lady decorator's appraisal. "It's perfectly *charming*," she said, "but where are your lights?" She was answered by the flipping of a switch, plunging the room into darkness.

My own favorite incandescent tools are the PAR 38, the R-40, and the T-10 reflector showcase lamps. "Slimline," among the fluorescents, gives longer tube lengths with smaller diameters, instant start, variety of intensities, and the substantial single contact base is a big improvement over the fragile bi-pin. "Circline" is a great help in bar and restaurant lighting where curves are a factor. Cold-cathode fluorescents are more useful in decorative and display applications than where visibility is a prime consideration (less lumen output per running foot). It also requires careful planning and installation for its high-voltage operation, but has the advantage of longer life, compared with hot cathodes. It is very satisfactory, in a variety of shapes, lengths and colors, for use in domes, coves, along curved partitions, and with dropped ceilings of various irregular shapes.

RESTAURANTS

THEY ARE PLANNED FOR FOOD AND FOR ATMOSPHERE

A SIMPLIFIED diagram of a restaurant would show a box with two open ends: one end would be the food-intake; the other would attract the customers. If the restaurant is planned well, food and customer — both properly prepared — will meet in the middle.

The intake of food and its preparation is a complex technical process, but it no longer holds many mysteries that can't be solved by clear thinking and fluent organization. The intake of customers, on the other hand, is almost a fine art, involving not only the best planning ability but also a smattering of showmanship and psychology. In the motor-city of Los Angeles, for example, "Mine Host" may virtually have to pry his customers off the fast concrete expressways which crisscross Southern California. He therefore sets up enormous neon-lighted billboard-façades, and his architect might as well become reconciled to them.

Supposing, however, that you have your customer where you want him, the next step is to decide exactly what you want to do with him. Some downtown cafeterias, for instance, try to get a complete rush-hour turnover of customers every 20 minutes; they will, therefore, be designed specifically to discourage loungers. Other restaurants, especially those that serve drinks, will try to hold their customers as long as they can; *their* atmosphere, therefore, is going to be calculated to soothe, comfort and detain. Some eating places, along highways and so on, don't depend upon "repeat" customers, while others count upon at least 50 per cent of their business to come from steady patrons.

How does one make "atmosphere"? The answer, according to one experienced restaurant designer, is to control everything from the lettering on your façade to the lettering on the customer's check. The first thing to decide is exactly *what* atmosphere the owner wants. Does he plan to attract a Hollywood, or a Colonial Dame? Does he propose to feed people waiting to board a Constellation, or to provide relaxation for a Board of Directors in a Downtown Club? Is he asking you to design a fluorescently brilliant cafeteria, or is he planning to serve home-cooked meals under home-like filament lamps? And, finally, where does he plan to build? Among semi-tropical California plant-life, or in the slick, brassy surroundings of Chicago's Loop? The answers to these questions will go to determine your atmosphere.

Lighting, especially, is one aspect of restaurant design that can't be overemphasized. When a Hollywood restaurant has its "Premiere," vast batteries of searchlights may be called into action to make the Battle of Britain look, by comparison, like a mild argument among friends; whereas an intimate little restaurant near Rockefeller Center may deliberately try to put up an almost shy front, dimly lit, to make its patrons feel that they have hit on something out of the ordinary and special. This same psychological approach can be used effectively in designing interior lighting: light that glosses over a woman's vital statistics may do a great deal to boost a restaurant's returns; while pinpoint spots that turn each table into an intimate little island may do the same and more.

Let's assume that all these factors have been considered and that the customer is happy and content. There still remains the primary question of a good plan. Apart from such obvious "musts" as interrupted circulation between kitchen and dining areas, easy control and plenty of space at the entrance, and comfortable table layout (all covered in detail in Building Types Study, see pages 150-172), we must deal with the all-important problem of fluent kitchen planning. Unless it is solved efficiently, your restaurant won't operate at a profit.

Kitchen areas generally fall into four groups: the receiving and storage area, the food preparation area, the pick-up area, the dishwashing area. In addition, there must be certain facilities for the restaurant staff — very important if you want it to give good service.

Kitchen equipment, materials and finishes used should be carefully selected, preferably with the help of a kitchen specialist. Materials and finishes must be chosen for cleanliness and hard wear, and floors must also be slipproof. Fire-resistance is a special consideration near the ranges, which will have hoods large enough to prevent the spread of fires, and must be supported on non-inflammable floors insulated with air spaces. Finally, and most importantly, the ventilating system of the kitchen as well as that of the entire restaurant must be perfect; occasionally two entirely separate systems are used for kitchen and dining areas.

From here on every restaurant owner and his architect are on their own. Their ability to solve each problem in its special setting will be the measure of their success.

AN EATING PLACE FOR MOTORIZED DINERS

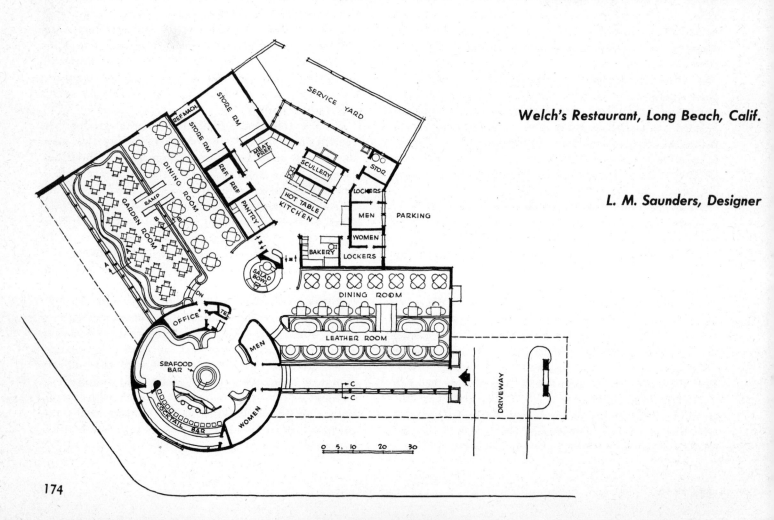

Welch's Restaurant, Long Beach, Calif.

L. M. Saunders, Designer

Maynard L. Parker Photos

IN SOME parts of the country, where eating out has become almost impossible without a car, restaurants must do two things they don't necessarily have to do elsewhere: they must attract the attention of relatively fast-moving motorists, and they must provide parking space for at least as many cars as they have tables.

Welch's in Long Beach does both of these things well. Few motorists could avoid spotting the fluted, cactus-green rotunda at the corner of San Antonio Drive and Atlantic Avenue. And once they have turned into the wide driveway they will find ample parking space.

It is interesting to note that even with a somewhat inflexible plan can go a rather free and elegant exterior, replete with long roof overhang, floor-to-ceiling windows of a single sheet of glass, free-standing lally column supports, and a pleasant integration of out- and indoor planting. The fact that the acceptance of such details is sometimes only skin-deep (as in this case) does not detract from the pleasing notion that practical businessmen — such as restaurant owners — seem to have discovered that good design pays. It may not be long before they discover that it pays in the plan too.

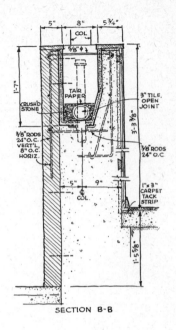

SECTION B-B

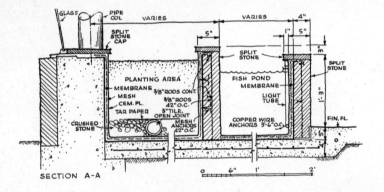

SECTION A-A

The Garden Room, perhaps the most successful part of this restaurant, has a spacious informality. Serpentine walls, originally used in America by Jefferson, have recently become popular again since Richard Neutra used them effectively in his Nesbit House.

The planning of the kitchen-dining relationship is generally sound, but the distance from the kitchen to the customer could have been shortened if the designer had been willing to give up the axial and symmetrical patterns underlying his plan. The overall architectural effect achieved in this room is nevertheless pleasant

Maynard L. Parker Photos

The kitchen is carefully planned. To the left, close to the waiters' return door, is the dishwashing area. Opposite it is the pick-up counter for orders prepared on the range at the extreme right. Refrigerator and meat-preparation are in the rear

Kramer Photo

The restaurant is jointly owned by a group of Navy officers who, presumably being fluent in Chinese, have inscribed the cocktail bar (left) with the rather gloomy motto: "Enjoy yourself, for it is later than you think!" The Dining Room (below) immediately adjoins the Garden Room. To the right is a large, terra-cotta colored "Salad Bowl"

Photos by Maynard L. Parker except where noted. Mural by Ernest Neuman

A long ramp serves as a pleasant waiting area and leads up from the main entrance at the driveway. The circular archway (allegedly Chinese) frames the aquarium-like seafood bar at the center of the building

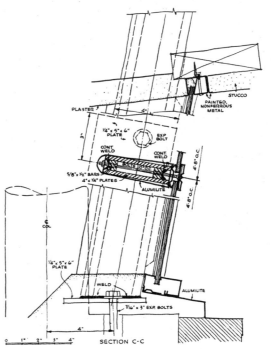

WINDOW DETAIL

The North Dining Room (below) reaches out from the central "Salad Bowl." It adjoins the Leather Room (lower right), which is more subdued in character than the opposite Garden Room. Its long tables are ingeniously designed to pivot on a fixed pedestal and swing out, so that diners can walk around to their seats rather than slide in sideways. The Leather Room overlooks the entrance ramp

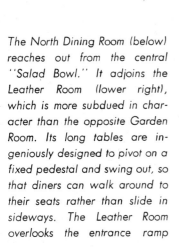

RESTAURANT KITCHENS

Material for this section was supplied by Herman H. Siegel, Architect; Harry Greitzer, Viking Kitchen Equipment Co.; Samuel Greenspan, Nathan Straus-Duparquet, Inc., with all photographs from the latter. Data on ventilation and air conditioning is from Peter Frank, Armo Cooling & Ventilating Co.

Reni Photos

Photo at right shows Garde Manger section in kitchen of the Mayflower Hotel, Washington, D. C., executed by Straus-Duparquet. Foreground: bread warmer behind, sea food bar

IT has been said that the restaurant architect's job is to attract customers; after that it is up to the operator to hang on to them with good food and service. But the architect has a manifest responsibility here, too. Bad planning in this department results not only in loss of custom, but in excessive china breakage, loss of silverware, spoiled food, actions by the Board of Health, and numerous vexations to the help, with consequent loss of their efficiency and even hire.

Essentially every kitchen area, for all restaurant types, conforms to certain basic requirements, and to an ideal plan of layout and relationships among the indispensable functions: receipt and storage of food, preparation, cooking, service, and utensilry washing. It is difficult, however, to be statistical regarding proportions of total area required for these operations to total dining space. It should be obvious from the preceding Building Types Study that require-

ments at Sakele's, offering full-course menus of wide selection, are vastly different from those in Tropical Gardens, where food is almost an incidental service to liquor. It is possible simply to say that kitchen and service areas, in currently successful operations, are occupying between 50 and 100 per cent the total area of dining spaces, with increasing tendency toward the top figure, to accommodate all the provisions recommended by experts for smooth efficiency.

First consideration, in establishing the layout and relationships of kitchen and service areas, must be unimpeded one-way traffic of all personnel. Waiters should enter the kitchen from dining areas, and leave by separate doors, ideally operating by "magic-eye" in the one necessary direction. A waiter entering from the dining room, presumably with a load of dirty dishes, should come immediately upon the washing section, where he deposits his tray, proceeding then to pick up new orders. Next in line

should be the *Garde Manger*, or salad, sandwich, cold meat and sea food section. After this, the Hot Food Area, adjacent to ranges and cooking equipment, followed by the dessert, pastry and beverage section, the last before return to the dining room. Preparation, storage and receipt areas should be entirely distinct from all the above, with the latter adjacent to outside delivery entrances. However, all sections, distinct or integrated, must be closely related for convenience and efficiency, preferably contiguous or with adequate means of vertical communication.

Basic equipment for the Dishwashing Area includes: shelves or ledges on the soiled dish table to rest trays for unloading; preliminary soaking sinks; pre-flushing equipment to carry off the loosened swill, permitting longer operation of washing machines without change of water. Glass washing equipment should be of the brush type, with a series of gentle slides below table level to assist in

Below, left: Hot Food Area in Mayflower kitchen, with warming units in close-up. Right: Mayflower dish and glass washing section, showing exhaust hoods over washing machines; stacking baskets for glasses. Service tables contain trays beneath

Reni Photo

Left: washing equipment in Restaurant of Namm's Dept. Store, Brooklyn; Morris Lapidus, Architect; kitchen, Straus-Duparquet:

Note soaking sink and pre-flush for swill. Right: Mayflower preparation equipment; note vegetable parer at far end of sinks

basket-stacking of glasses as they emerge from the washer. A silver-washing machine is now available which cleans by means of a revolving barrel, filled with small metal pellets. In addition, this equipment sterilizes and burnishes, requiring no drying.

Efficient new equipment for the *Garde Manger* section includes mechanically refrigerated units for salad, cold meats and sea food, to be hooked in very economically with the main refrigeration system. Of great advantage here, as in other pick-up sections, are counter-weighted units permitting the stacking within of dishes and trays; only the top two or three protrude above table level, regardless of the many or few pushing up from beneath. These units can be cooled or heated, and insure minimum

exposure of the dishes or trays contained.

For the Hot Food Area, incessant refinements in pressure cookers and kettles, baking and roasting ovens are more and more obtainable. Units to keep food warm until serving are almost indispensable; one type of shelf unit, for installation above the cook's table, is designed to hold complete orders. Its upper tier has an insulated core and convex bottom, returning heat from the lower tier on which the food is placed. Removable grease filters in range hoods are a great convenience in this section.

General provisions for kitchen and service areas should include: rounded corners and cove bases; welded stainless-steel surfaces (nuts and bolts are great dirt collectors); ramps in place of steps, if changes in level cannot possibly be

avoided; impervious floors, walls, and even ceilings (see discussion of materials, pages 151-157); floor drains for daily hosings; at least 20 f.c. of light at working levels; such conveniences, where possible, as walk-in boxes with electrical germ-killing devices and magic-eye operation; and, of course, such employee-morale maintainers as locker-toilet-rest-room facilities and adequate ventilation in all regions.

Ventilation and Air Conditioning

Prime purposes of a restaurant's ventilating system are the removal of foul air and heat from kitchen areas, and the prevention of these in dining spaces. Bad-air exhaustion should take place as close as possible to points of origin. Range hoods preferably should be no more than 6 ft. above the floor; dishwashing machines should have hoods over each opening. Construction of all hoods should be such that there is a narrow curtain of high velocity air around the exhaust perimeter.

With any extensive exhaust system, a positive supply of replacement air must be provided (relying for this, to any considerable degree, on haphazard filtration through doors and windows, makes many difficulties). A controlled-intake balance should provide a little more air supplied than exhausted in dining areas, with the reverse holding for kitchens. This maintains a slight flow of air from the dining areas, in one direction toward the kitchen to repel odors, and in the other toward the street, to prevent drafts. Also, this replacement air should be heated. One method is simply preheating to room temperature, for preventing cold drafts; another is to make it the principal heat carrier, eliminating radiators. Protective measures

Below, left: Mayflower cooking equipment; soup kettle in left foreground; behind, pressure vegetable cooker; at right is box for prepared fish, with small drawer for scallops, etc. Photo at right shows unit for booth-service utensils, coffee, water, etc. at Namm's

George W. Nuckols Photo

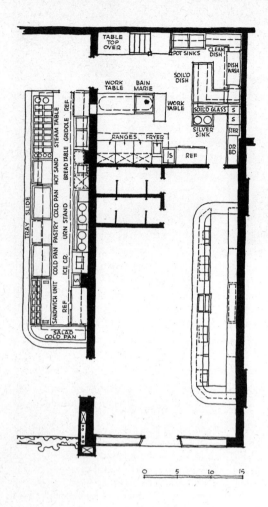

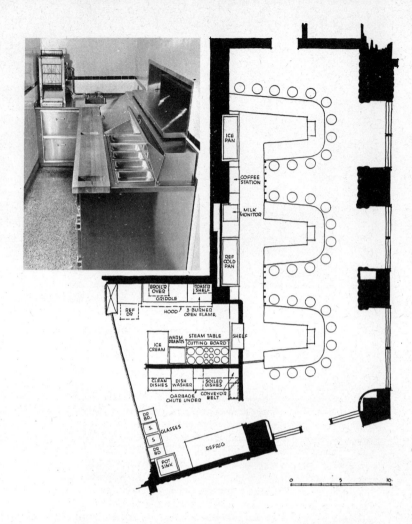

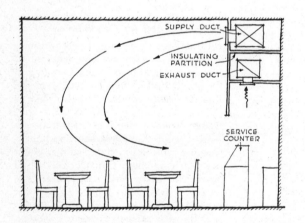

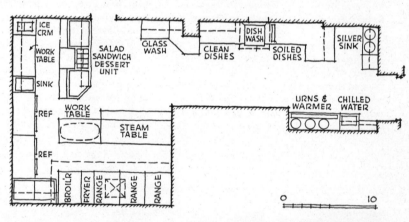

Plan top, left, is kitchen and counter layout in Reed's Cafeteria (see also pages 153 and 160). Inset photo at top, right, with plan of Riker's (see also page 170), is actually equipment at Namm's, but illustrates means of intercommunication between counter and kitchen, essential to this type of operation. Drawing directly above, left, shows prevention of "short circuiting" in operating air conditioning with counter-hood exhaust. Plan at right, directly above, is kitchen of Field's Restaurant and bar (see also pages 152-160)

must be taken to prevent freezing of heating-coil condensate at below 32° F.

Air-conditioning factors vary according to restaurant types. It is possible that in self-service and counter operations, temperature and humidity will be kept at lower general levels of difference, between inside and outside, than in restaurants where patrons stay longer.

Automatic control is very important, particularly in cafeterias and luncheonettes, with their rapid changes of occupancy and short, heavy loads during peak periods. To meet these fluctuations, compressors are probably the type of refrigeration source most generally used.

It is usually good practice, when external conditions warrant, to use outside air *entirely* for conditioning systems. Otherwise, just enough outside air is introduced to maintain the balances described previously, with the main body recirculated. Replaceable-type filters are most practical for both air conditioning and ventilating purposes.

Inlets for air-conditioning and ventilation must be calculated carefully, not only to avoid drafts but to prevent short-circuiting of air-circulation to exhaust openings. Also general architectural schemes must be studied for harmony of outlets with room shapes and seating plans. A harmonious example, in this respect, is illustrated on page 155.

Hedrich-Blessing Photos

A LIGHTING EFFECT FOR EVERY MOOD

Henrici's Restaurant, Merchandise Mart, Chicago

James F. Eppenstein & Raymond Schwab, Architects

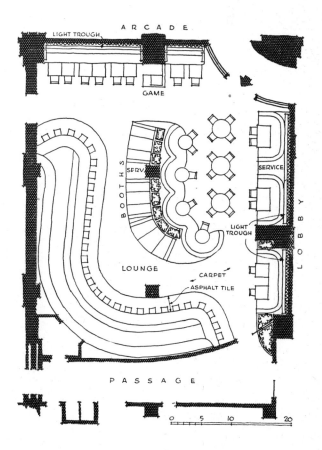

OFF THE ARCADE in Chicago's Merchandise Mart, Henrici's Restaurant presents an unexpected vision of glamour. Designed around a colorful mural by Felix Ruvalo and an intricate lighting system that changes in intensity for luncheon, cocktails and dinner, this elegant little retreat is said to wow the customers.

While there is nothing revolutionary about the plan (which has clearly been dictated by existing conditions), colors and lighting raise some interesting points. Throughout the restaurant various shades of green predominate. While the mural may seem aggressively restless, its color scheme has been recalled in the furnishings and thus subordinated to the overall architectural effect. The lighting system uses pin-hole spots, recessed ceiling fixtures and theater-type dimmers.

Among the lighting tricks used in Henrici's is a trough that illuminates the rich wall draperies woven with a glittering gold thread. At lunch time the overall lighting will be of high intensity; for afternoon cocktails the intensity is reduced until, at dinner time, a dim, intimate lighting prevails. The plant island to the right has its own spot illumination

A view from the Arcade shows the large, clean frame of the doors, set into a curved glass wall that permits clear vision of the interior. The recessed box lighting in the ceiling seems to detract somewhat from the tranquil, overall effect. Exterior is of Italian travertine marble

Hedrich-Blessing Photos

Ruvalo's luminescent mural is stressed by ''black light'' to become the dominant feature of the restaurant. The lighting of the bartenders' work area is below customer eye-level to cut out un-pleasant glare. In the rear, at the turn of the long curve, there is a service hatch for outside supplies

REDEVELOPED
WITH A FLAIR

First Step in Scheme for Palm Springs Corp.,
Palm Springs, Calif.

A. Quincy Jones, Jr., Architect;
Paul R. Williams, Associate

IN this restaurant's first season, customers were
so successfully drawn into the interior court
and surrounding shops that the owners of the
property are now trying to speed up the remodeling of the entire block. As the photographs on
these four pages show, considerable flair and
flavor were used to good effect as a customer lure.

The new restaurant building was the first step
in the remodeling project. Its design was complicated by the fact that the existing foundation
and basement had to be used, and also by the
leases already signed with four different types of
tenant. The building houses the Town and
Country Restaurant, the offices of "The Desert
Sun," Palm Springs' newspaper, and three shops,
plus the offices of the Palm Springs Corporation,
owners of the property, and four small apartments. Exterior walls are cement plaster and
redwood; interior walls are plaster, redwood and
Roman brick; ceilings are acoustically treated.
Framing is steel.

Completion of the entire project originally was
expected to take two or three years and called
for a careful construction schedule. To avoid
even brief interruption of business, as one section
is finished, a tenant from an untouched section
is moved into it to make way for further remodeling or rebuilding.

Julius Shulman Photos

Spark of the redevelopment scheme is the atmosphere-packed patio leading to the Town & Country Restaurant. The restaurant building, first one completed under the plan, houses also offices and shops, and has four small apartments on second floor (see plan, next page)

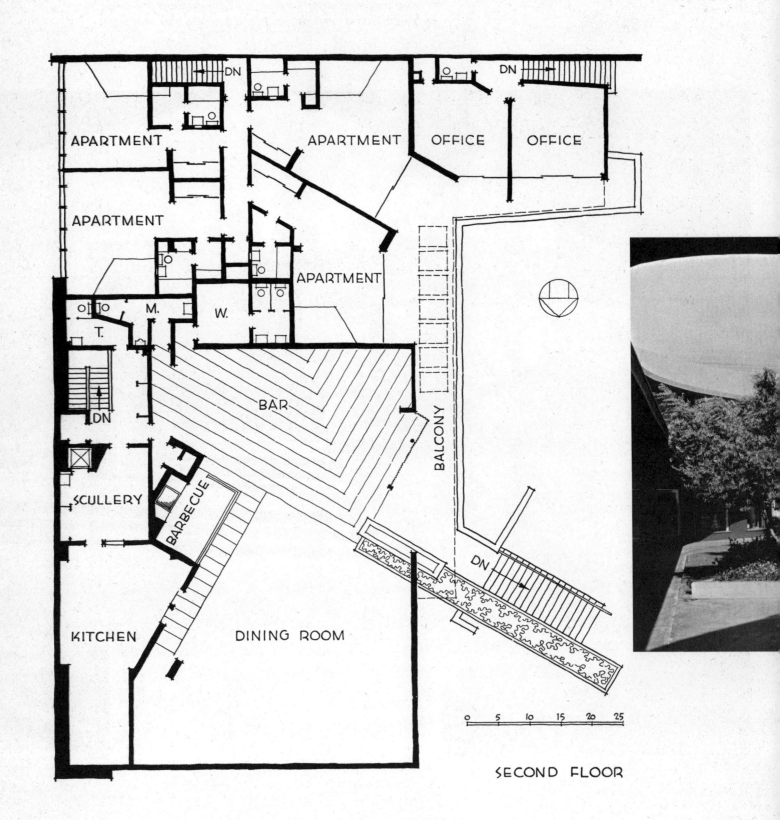

APARTMENT

APARTMENT

APARTMENT

OFFICE

OFFICE

DN

DN

M.

W.

T.

BALCONY

BAR

DN

SCULLERY

BARBECUE

KITCHEN

DINING ROOM

DN

0   5   10   15   20   25

SECOND FLOOR

The second-floor apartments have their own entrance from Indian Avenue along the south side of the block, but shops and restaurant face the court (opposite page). Commercial tenants are varied, including the local newspaper, and three different types of store

Julius Shulman Photos

Cortlandt V. D. Hubbard

RESTAURANT PLANNED FOR SELF-SERVICE

Longleys Restaurant

New York City

Joseph G. Morgan, Architect

Thomas F. Hennessy, Associate Architect

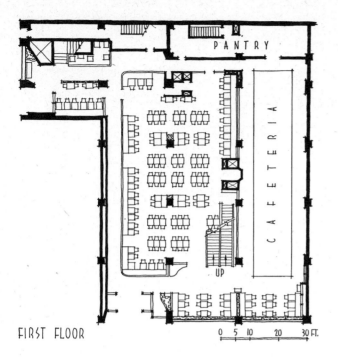

FIRST FLOOR   0 5 10   20   30 FT.

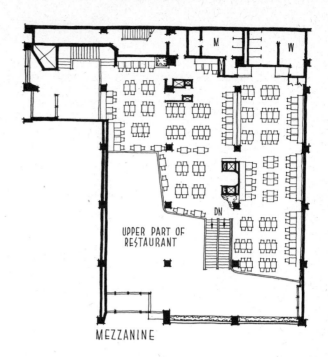

MEZZANINE

THE PROBLEM HERE was to fit a smoothly working self-service restaurant into an existing building. Located opposite Radio City, the property is L-shaped, fronting both on Sixth Avenue and on busy 50th Street. To accommodate the rapid turnover during peak periods, the service station is an island; customers pass along it on either side, passing checker and cashier at end; each line can serve 10 per minute. The flow of customer traffic is kept completely out of the dining area.

A seating capacity of 500 was made possible by the introduction of a balcony seating 300. The low ceiling heights which resulted are minimized visually by indirect lighting panels forming a pattern of 8-ft squares. The irregular shape of the balcony and the open railing of plastic tiller rope and steel also help to counterbalance the low ceilings.

RESTAURANT PLANNED

FOR SELF-SERVICE

Public areas are covered with a variety of plastics, completely washable, and with warm tones of brick and wood to blend with huge mural by Cobelle on south wall. Stairs are broad and low, balcony rail is open to help attract customers to upper level

Cortlandt V. D. Hubbard

This section of the study on drive-in buildings was prepared in joint collaboration of Architectural Record and Restaurant Management, in which it also appears

Drive-in restaurants include a vast range of establishments, from hamburger stands to elaborate coffee shops, dining and banquet rooms and cocktail lounges. Some cater solely to motorists, with no interior seating, others provide large parking areas for interior service. The success of all can be fostered by careful planning. Apart from good food, success factors include: adequate parking, attractive surroundings, service efficiency, and employee welfare.

Surroundings and menu should be determined by the type of clientele to be served. Tastes of business people

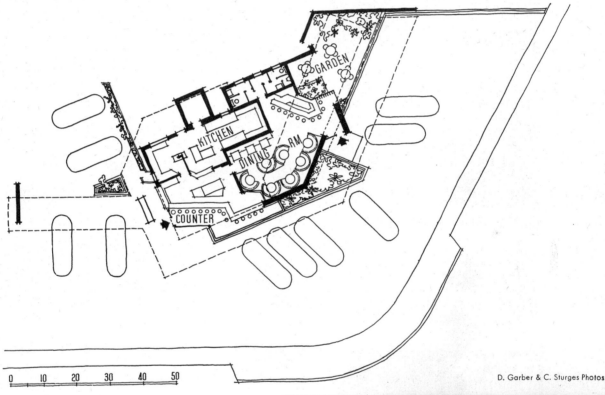

D. Garber & C. Sturges Photos

Henry's Drive-In Restaurant, Glendale, Calif.; John Lautner, Architect. Layout shows good organization of the various elements; drive-in facilities (at left in plan and photo, right) are clearly separated from those of dining room and bar. Car-hop service is well sheltered by roofs and overhangs. Garden room (top photograph and plan above) takes advantage of California climate, provides cool retreat for afternoon cocktails. Structural elements have been expressed frankly as decorative devices. Kitchen and behind-counter service areas are centrally located for all food service; deliveries may be made conveniently from rear of building. Good visibility is assured sign by elevating it on tower above building

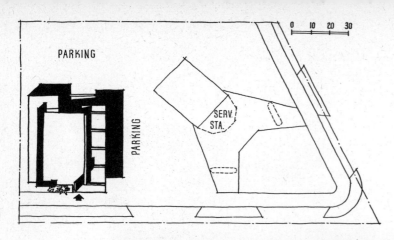

Biff's Restaurant, Hollywood, Calif.; Douglas Honnald, Architect. Extensive glass areas and well studied lighting are used to attract customers to this compact restaurant. Solid brick mass of service areas provides visual, as well as actual, anchorage for lean-to steel framing members of lunch room structure

George R. Szanik Photo

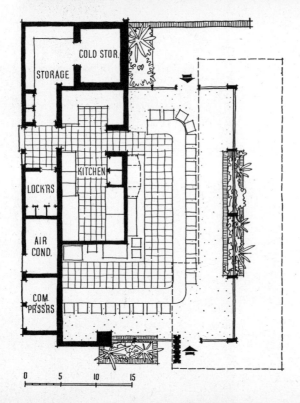

Van de Kamp's Restaurant (right), Los Angeles, Calif.; Wayne McAllister, Architect. Service speed and capacity of the drive-in are doubled by use of twin facilities: two service areas, two short order kitchens, two dishwashing rooms and a two-way walk-in refrigerator. Tile and stainless steel surfaces make kitchen (second from top) easy to clean. Special tray racks are loaded directly from dishwashing room. Pick-up counter (bottom) is fitted with all necessary service items. Coffee shop is located in an adjacent building

vary from those of families with children, shoppers or plant workers. Some locations will attract different people at different hours. A full menu requires large kitchens for preparation, large parking areas because of time required for consumption. Areas can be minimized by limiting choice of foods. Profit requires frequent customer turnover: convenient layouts and time-saving devices can speed food preparation and service. Labor costs can be cut if areas can be closed in slack periods.

SIZE AND LOCATION OF SITE

Size of plot depends on type and extent of facilities provided: minimum is probably 150 by 150 ft, preferably on a corner. A wide frontage is best for visibility and ease of access. Inadequate parking can create ill will. Inclusion of dining rooms, bars, etc., requires proportionately larger space.

Relationship to neighborhood: Select site which will have stable year-round patronage from near-by business, shopping or industrial centers. A low cost area toward which business is moving, or the outskirts of a dense residential area, is often advantageous. Zoning ordinances should be checked for possible changes. Check availability of such services as: sewage disposal, rubbish removal, electricity, city phones, laundry, equipment repair, food and ice supplies.

Relationship to highways: Site should be on a major traffic artery, plainly visible from a distance, and so situated that traffic can easily stop and approach property from both directions. Check for highway changes.

PLOT LAYOUT

Parking areas: Entrances, exits, and parking spaces should be clearly marked to assure maximum capacity and prevent road block. Use easily maintained surfacing; a dark color will cut down glare. The area should slope only enough for drainage; say, $\frac{1}{4}$ in. to the ft. Separate drive-in parking from that of dining areas. Set apart areas for deliveries, and for trucks and busses, if such patronage is expected.

Service walks: Allow for car bumper overhang on walks adjacent to buildings; raise about 6 in. Radiant heat is sometimes used for snow melting and for comfort of car-hops on chill evenings.

Weather protection: Canopies shelter car-hops from rain and glare. An overhang 18 ft wide will protect service to all car doors. Other methods: fixed or sliding awnings on metal frames; column-supported roofs.

Terraces and landscaping: Take full advantage of any pleasant view. Outdoor terraces or gardens with tables can be attractive and profitable; many motorists like to get out and "stretch their legs." Trees used for shade should not hamper traffic.

GENERAL PLANNING

Plans: All elements should radiate from central kitchens. Each should have separate service-ports into

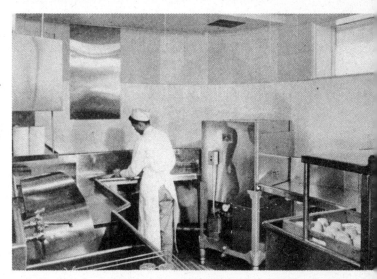

Tile Council of America

kitchen, an exterior entrance, plainly marked on outside, and interior intercommunication.

Kitchens: Group together all equipment for each operation. Allow aisles wide enough for easy passage with loaded trays. "In" and "out" doors will speed service. A rear entry should be included for deliveries and garbage removal. Labor costs can be cut if layout permits one cook to handle kitchen during quiet hours.

Dishwashing area: Locate area convenient to car-hops, counter, dining areas and kitchen; conceal from the public. Pass doors for depositing soiled dishes, and for picking up clean ones will speed service.

Pick-up counter: Allow pick-up space for 50 per cent of car-hops at one time; the average car-hop can handle 6 cars. Automatic doors ease service. Wings at each side

Rettig's Restaurant, Houston, Texas; MacKie & Kamrath, Architects. An interplay of wood forms and textures produce an arresting, easily identified building. Setbacks in plan permit window for each booth. Service drive is adjacent to kitchen, routes delivery trucks away from customer parking. Location of entrances permits close supervision of all areas

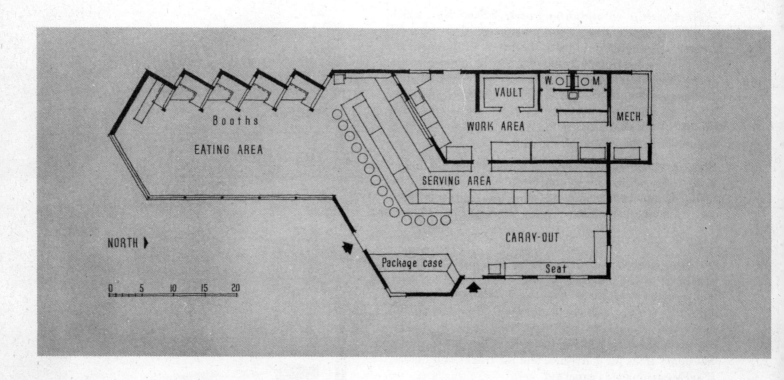

of counter should contain service set-ups, trays and water. Counter men should be able to reach kitchen passport, coffee urns, malt mixers, fountain and refrigerated bottle box.

Cashier's desk: If checking is done as food is delivered to car-hops, cash register should be located in pick-up space. With one cashier and both interior and car-hop service, the desk should be convenient to each and near entry for control and supervision. In small drive-ins, records might be kept here; in large concerns, a separate office is needed.

Counter service: A minimum of 30 to 36 in. clear aisle must be left behind counters. Turnover is faster and cost of operation less with counter seats than with tables. When combined with dining rooms, counters should be nearest entrance. Counter-high pass windows and a

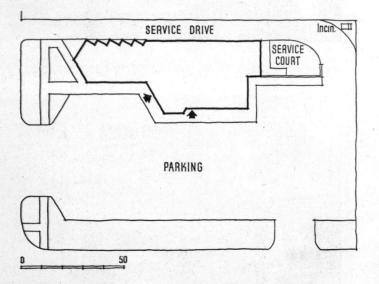

central entrance to kitchen from behind counter are desirable. Part of counter might be devoted to dining room service.

Dining rooms: Side tables should be provided with equipment for all set-ups, and with soiled linen hoppers. The most flexible table layout uses 2-seat tables, combined for groups. Booths use more space, but are preferred by some customers. Extensive dining areas require extra pantries and equipment. Protect diners against heat, moisture and sounds from kitchen.

Storage rooms: Provide for food, supply and equipment storage of all types, near delivery entrances. Protect overhead waste and water lines against drip. Cleaning equipment should be apart from food processes.

Wash rooms: Toilets should open from inside and out-

End wall extends at angles above building to provide unified base for restaurant signs

Mears Studio Photos

side where there is drive-in service. Large concerns need separate rooms for employees, with lockers for coats and changes of uniform located near by.

Waist-high windows allow use of built-in seats along outer wall, still permit interior and exterior views

CONSTRUCTION AND FINISHES

Construction: Climate and fire hazards are important in establishing type of construction. Many cities require fireproof materials.

Finishes should be durable and easy to keep up. Sanitation is one of the most serious problems; state and local regulations must be followed.

Periodic modernization of building may be necessary; construction should be adaptable.

Floors: Tile, Terazzo, concrete or composition make good floors. Avoid surfaces which are slippery when

wet. Wooden slat floors in service areas should be recessed flush with floor, removable for scrubbing.

Walls: Surfaces of walls should be washable. Simple decoration is usually preferred. Plants, lighting, mirrors and color provide accent.

Counter and table tops: Materials should not discolor, scratch or chip easily. They should stand up under heavy usage and be easy to clean. Plastics, tile, linoleum and wood make good surfaces.

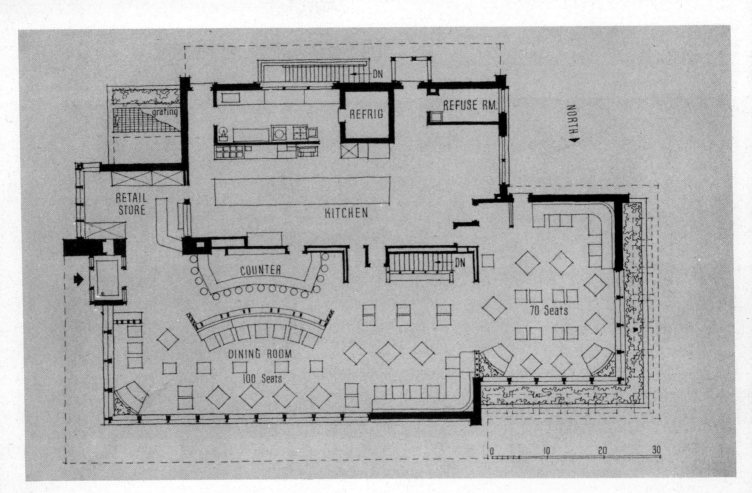

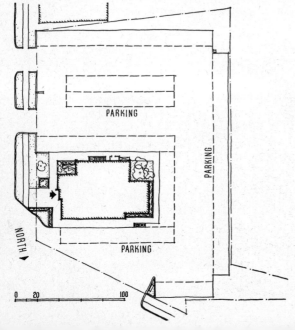

DESIGN AND PROMOTIONAL FEATURES

Visibility: A successful restaurant must attract motorists from a distance by signs, colors and illumination. A tower serves as a commanding billboard. Dining areas should be made visible from exterior by use of glass and illumination. Lights should never shine directly into the eyes of patrons.

Architectural treatment: It is best to avoid a superficial treatment; frank expression of structure can often make an arresting design. Standardized treatments are useful for identification of a chain.

Advertising features: Dishes, trays, uniforms, windshield cards, menus and sales books can be good advertising if well designed. Many drive-ins feature entertain-

Hot Shoppes Restaurant, Philadelphia, Pa.; Joseph Morgan, Architect. Design, both interior and exterior, expresses quiet, comfortable dining. Sense of privacy is given to interior spaces by screen partition enclosing lunch counter and folding wall between dining areas (below). Glare is controlled by overhangs, trees and thin curtains at windows. Retail shop sells food specialties to take out. Curb service is offered to motorists at rear of building

Cortlandt V. D. Hubbard Photos

ment, sometimes staged on the roof, as added customer inducement.

EQUIPMENT

Food preparation equipment should be of sanitary construction, easily taken apart for cleaning, and with no lead or cadmium plated parts. Electrical machines should be of same voltage. Depending on menu, kitchens should include: preparation table, broiler, fryer, range, griddle, work table, sink, refrigerator, sandwich unit, range hood and exhaust fan, food warmer, service pick-up table with refrigerator below, ice cream cabinet.

To facilitate car service, a microphone might be used to place orders; a light panel with waitresses' numbers signals when orders are ready.

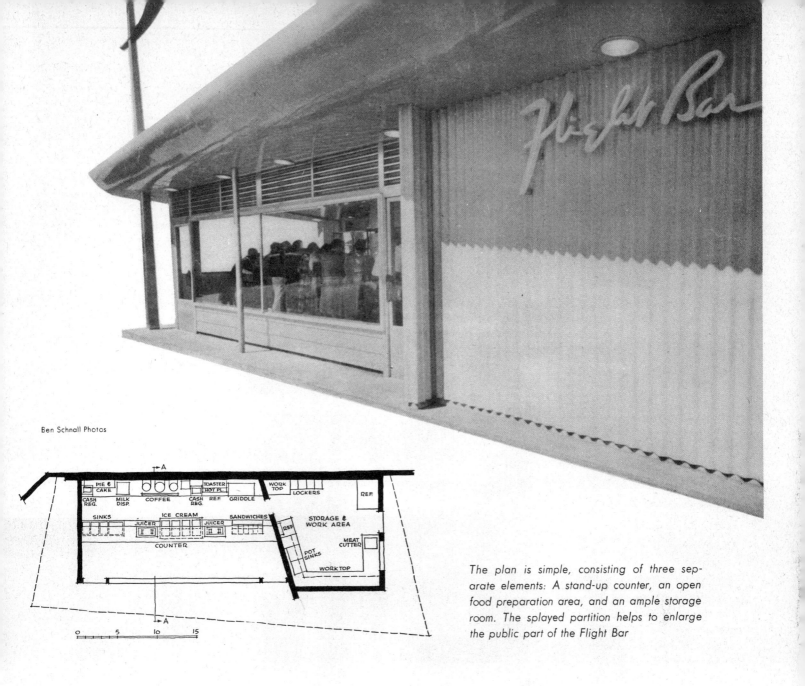

Ben Schnall Photos

The plan is simple, consisting of three separate elements: A stand-up counter, an open food preparation area, and an ample storage room. The splayed partition helps to enlarge the public part of the Flight Bar

A SNACK BETWEEN LANDING AND TAKE-OFF

FLIGHT BAR, LA GUARDIA AIRPORT   *NEW YORK*

Lester C. Tichy

Architect

IN THIS sleek, aluminum-finished Flight-Bar at New York's La Guardia Airport, Lester Tichy has projected his successful railroad design ideas into the business of air travel. Against the heavy, rather sterile formalism of the International Terminal Building, this bright and cheerful snack bar stands out well — as clearly a part of the air age as any transatlantic Clipper circling overhead. Designed to be completely demountable, the building's footing can be cut immediately below the two wide flange sections upon which it rests, and the whole structure may then be loaded upon trucks and moved to a new location. Thus the Flight Bar is in reality almost airborne: the airplane wing type of roof, the tall mast with its fin symbolizing air currents, and the finely polished aluminum detail are all designed to emphasize its modern character.

The storage room is encased in a corrugated asbestos-cement wall, while the Flight Bar itself has aluminum siding up to a low sill height, then large sheets of glass topped by continuous strips of aluminum louvers. Note the free-shaped push panel at the door

Ben Schnall Photos

Since it is not strictly part of the International Terminal, the Flight Bar must compete with the heavy façade of the Main Building. It does this without being offensive. Its roof-line, for example, follows the general level of the Main Building's entrance canopy, and its slanted edge points in the direction of the main traffic flow. The Flight Bar was designed for the Port of New York Authority, with whose kind permission it is published here

RESTAURANTS

Prepared in collaboration with **Restaurant Management**

WHAT RESTAURANT OWNERS THINK ABOUT

*By James S. Warren, **Editor**, **Restaurant Management***

CATERING to the public taste, both literally and figuratively, is the business of the restaurant owner. He is chiefly concerned, in his own thinking, with providing his customers with well-prepared, efficiently served meals in sufficient quantity to yield a maximum profit. He is vitally concerned with every phase of his business and he handles most of the details himself, from menu planning to purchasing raw materials, even cooking them, and supervising the daily routine throughout his entire establishment, as well as keeping a careful eye on the cash register. In most cases he owns his own business and is proud of the fact.

For these reasons he is realistic and tight fisted. He must see clearly a profit return on every investment he makes, whether in produce, personnel, equipment, or plan and design. He is usually much less interested, for example, in the esthetics of the decorative scheme than in a plan layout which will save his waitresses a few steps or serve more customers comfortably. He is keenly interested in every sales-stimulating, money-saving aspect of his business. For the most part he is thoroughly representative of the "small businessman" so much in the public eye and economic mind, and there are some 150,000 of him. Right now his pockets are bulging with money just earned

which he is itching to spend—providing he can be convinced that its spending will be an investment that will pay a proportionate yield.

For these reasons also he prefers to deal with an architect who understands the operation of the restaurant business, one who can talk with him in his own language, an architect who understands the problems of food delivery, food storage, preparation and cooking, who understands the integration and proportioning of the various services and areas, such as storerooms, kitchens, and dining rooms.

The architect, therefore, who can see the restaurateur's problem as a whole and in detail, and can offer suggestions on every phase of the business, as well as on the design and color of the dining room, will be best able to render profitable service in this field. The architect who can talk intelligently in terms of kitchen layout and equipment with the restaurant owner is likely to be most convincing and best able to influence him in constructive design ideas for both interior and exterior. So the function of the architect, to be successful in this field, is to cater to the purposes, pride, and prejudice of the restaurant owner by contributing materially to the efficiency, economy, and profit of the entire project.

HIGHWAY RESTAURANT for a 100-octane world

Francis R. Keally, Architect

ALTHOUGH this highway restaurant for the newly motorized world was designed especially for this Building Types Study, Mr. Keally is prepared to resent any suggestion that there is anything visionary about it. It is in fact, he points out, not unlike one he is doing right now for a client.

It exhibits, nevertheless, the imagination of an architect applied to a practical problem. Two features are especially noteworthy—the herb garden with dining tables around its perimeter, and the barbecue stockade. The barbecue pit is already a recognized feature of many highway eating places, especially in the West. But so often it is just a big grill standing by itself in a paper-littered side yard, its appetizing appeal further diluted by dust. Here it becomes a feature of an outdoor dining "stockade" visible alike from the highway and from the dining porch and main restaurant. The herb garden contributes further outdoor dining space, also visual interest from the principal dining room, not to mention the material for appealing sauces.

The visual service kitchen, to be done with a Dutch kitchen effect, is still another eye-catcher. But it has its distinctly practical side, for it keeps the waitresses in constant view of their customers, assuring the latter that the girls are not idly chatting in the kitchen.

If winters are cold the establishment automatically withdraws into its shell with the closing of outdoor areas and screened porch. Then perhaps the principal business would be done in the lunch counter, which is placed off by itself for the steady and profitable service of truck drivers and others who ride the roads the year 'round.

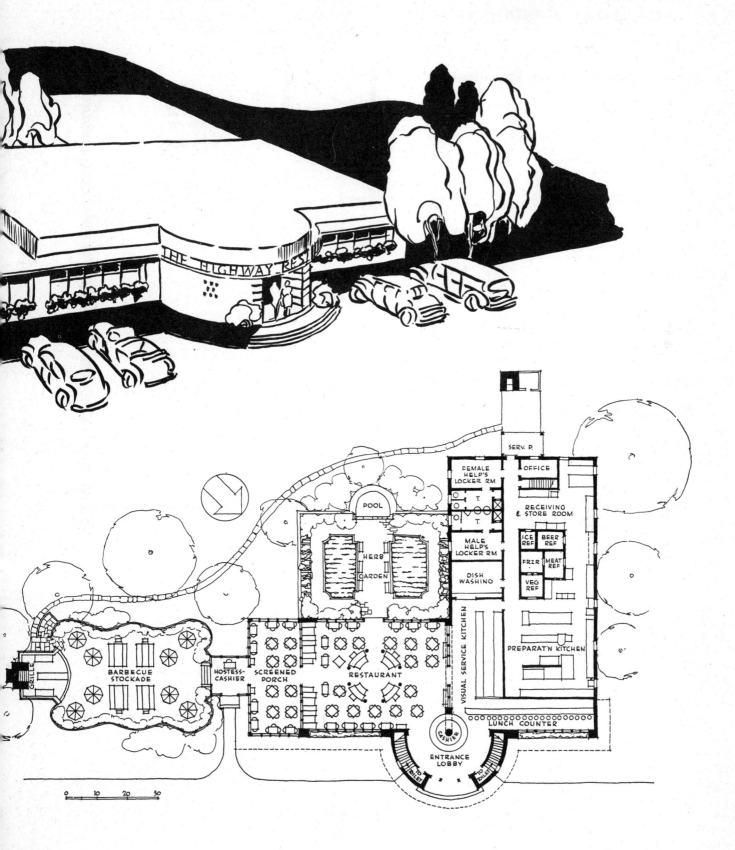

The cashier, just within the lobby space, has visual control
of all dining areas, also of the serving kitchen and the dishwashing room. Kitchen has been scientifically designed
by Arthur W. Dana, kitchen consultant (see next page)

Kitchen Plan for Highway Restaurant

Arthur W. Dana, Restaurant Consultant

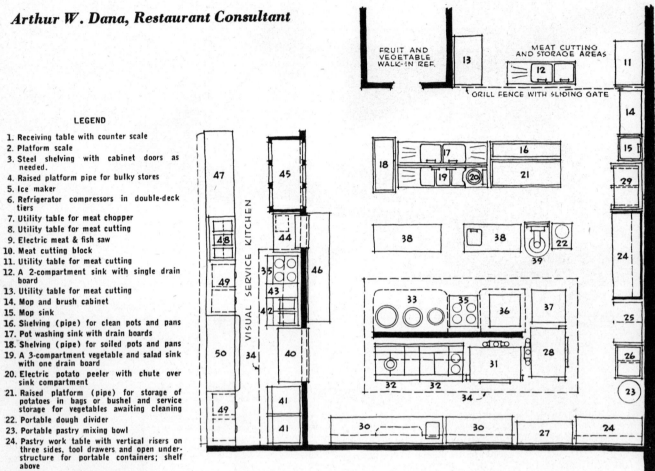

LEGEND

1. Receiving table with counter scale
2. Platform scale
3. Steel shelving with cabinet doors as needed.
4. Raised platform pipe for bulky stores
5. Ice maker
6. Refrigerator compressors in double-deck tiers
7. Utility table for meat chopper
8. Utility table for meat cutting
9. Electric meat & fish saw
10. Meat cutting block
11. Utility table for meat cutting
12. A 2-compartment sink with single drain board
13. Utility table for meat cutting
14. Mop and brush cabinet
15. Mop sink
16. Shelving (pipe) for clean pots and pans
17. Pot washing sink with drain boards
18. Shelving (pipe) for soiled pots and pans
19. A 3-compartment vegetable and salad sink with one drain board
20. Electric potato peeler with chute over sink compartment
21. Raised platform (pipe) for storage of potatoes in bags or bushel and service storage for vegetables awaiting cleaning
22. Portable dough divider
23. Portable pastry mixing bowl
24. Pastry work table with vertical risers on three sides, tool drawers and open understructure for portable containers; shelf above
25. Proofing cabinet with electric evaporator
26. Portable pastry rack
27. Storage cabinet with sliding doors
28. Double deck baking oven
29. Baker's refrigerator
30. Cook's tables; one to have sink and overhead pan rack; shelf above and slatted shelves below; tool drawers
31. Double deck roasting oven
32. Range tops (skeleton without oven, but with back panel and d.d. upper shelf)
33. Three steam-jacketed kettles, 30-gal., 15-gal. and 10-gal. capacities set in recessed trough
34. Overhead ventilating hood with grease filters

35. Open top range with oven below and d.d. shelf above
36. Vegetable steamer with 3 compartments
37. Vegetable and salad work table with utility sink
38. Vegetable and salad table with food chopper and French-fry cutter
39. 60-30 qt. electric mixer
40. Food and dish warmer with shelf doors on both long sides
41. Heavy duty gas broiler
42. Twin gas deep-fat fryer with shelf above
43. Spreader plate and shelves below and above

44. Utility table, pass-thru window and sink below
45. Reach-in refrigerator with doors on two sides
46. Utility table
47. Dessert and salad service counter with shelves below
48. Ice cream cabinet with service shelf above
49. Counter height refrigerator with work top and four refrigerator drawers
50. Electric hot food table with six interchangeable panel insets, service shelf above, cutting board

HAVING selected menu patterns and analyzed kitchen equipment requirements in terms of quantities of food (see ARCHITECTURAL RECORD, July, 1945, p. 72) the kitchen planner is ready to work out the most efficient system and layout. Here the receiving, storage and meat-cutting areas are separate from the kitchen itself (that's why the first 10 items of the legend are missing from the plan), for better control of costly merchandise, also here to serve the barbecue kitchen.

Vegetable preparation (Items 16-21) is simplified by having storage racks adjacent to the sink, and pot and pan storage near the pot-cleaning sink. High pressure vegetable cooking is facilitated by providing an open top range (35) and a utility sink (37) for cooling the cookers. Double-deck roasting ovens (31) separate from range tops (32) give good accessibility and convenient heights. Work space directly opposite is very important (30). The visual service kitchen includes: food and dish warming cabinets, gas broilers, deep fat fryers, open-top range for sauteing and frying, utility table and sink, and refrigerator. On the front counter are refrigerator drawers, electric hot food table, salad counter and ice cream cabinets.

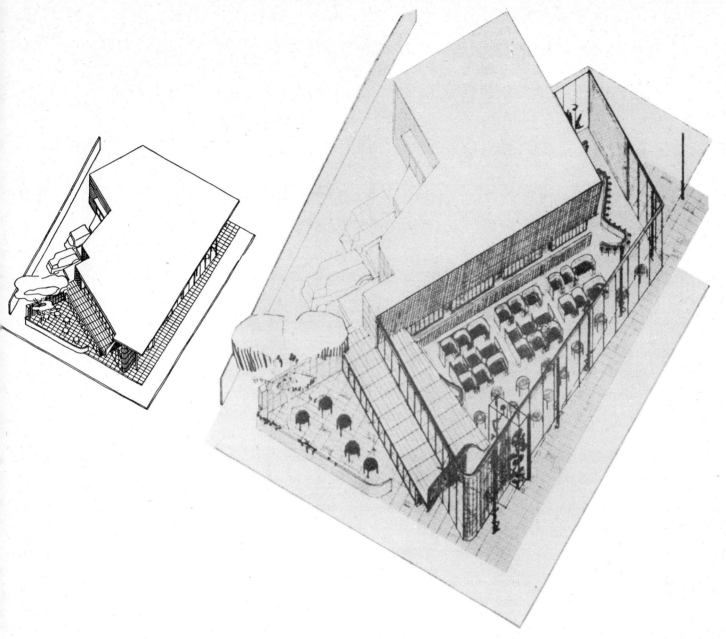

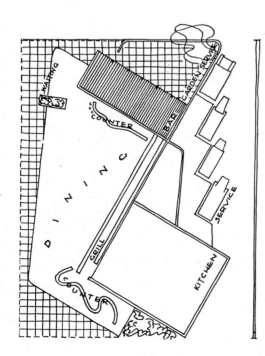

ANALYSIS OF RESTAURANT SPACE AND LAYOUT

Sumner Spaulding, Architect

Architectural design involves many factors, not the least of which is that of analyzing the client's problem and presenting a number of possible solutions, so that they can be compared on a practical, economic, and operating basis. The studies here shown are a portion of the analysis made by the architect in order to help the owner to come to a realistic decision as to the amount of space needed for the operation of his restaurant, and also the layout of that space in such a way as to provide both maximum attractiveness for his clients and maximum operating efficiency.

Two sets of studies were made: one, on a lot which measures 135 feet by 60 feet. The second scheme shows the possibility of

Cut-away aerial perspective and plan of scheme for "G" which helped the owner to visualize his projected building. Various schemes for single and double lot coverage are shown on the following pages

The diagram of functions and services was set up as a preliminary to the schematic plans for a restaurant covering the two lots, which are shown across the bottom of the page. At the right are the diagrams showing the plan schemes developed for the single lot.

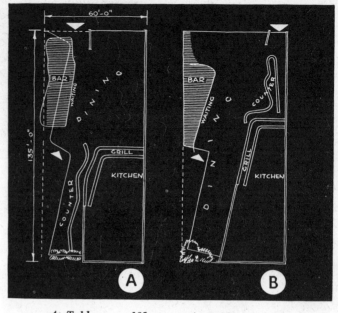

At Tables	135	At Tables	170
At Counters	35	At Counters	35
At Bar	24	At Bar	24
Tables at Bar	25	Tables at Bar	25

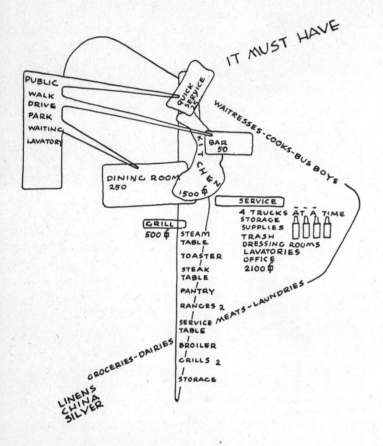

using an additional adjacent lot of almost the same size. The new restaurant building is to house one of the oldest and most popular restaurants in Beverly Hills. The present location is at the important intersection of Wilshire Boulevard and Santa Monica Boulevard.

The architect has worked out a list of requirements for this particular restaurant, and that is expressed in graphic form in the diagram, which shows what "it must have." The diagram separates the various functions and shows their interrela-

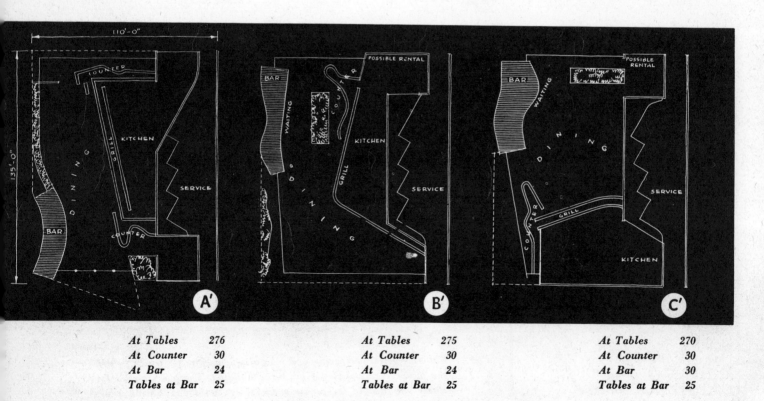

At Tables	276	At Tables	275	At Tables	270
At Counter	30	At Counter	30	At Counter	30
At Bar	24	At Bar	24	At Bar	30
Tables at Bar	25	Tables at Bar	25	Tables at Bar	25

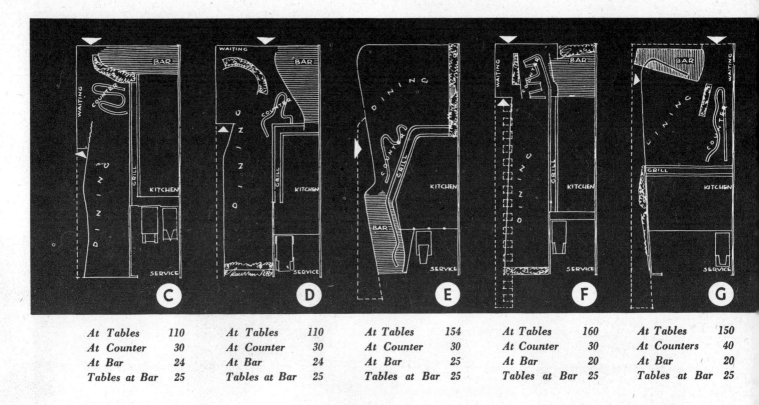

	C		D		E		F		G
At Tables	110	At Tables	110	At Tables	154	At Tables	160	At Tables	150
At Counter	30	At Counter	30	At Counter	30	At Counter	30	At Counters	40
At Bar	24	At Bar	24	At Bar	25	At Bar	20	At Bar	20
Tables at Bar	25	Tables at Bar	25	Tables at Bar	25	Tables at Bar	25	Tables at Bar	25

tionships, based on the predetermined requirements of a restaurant seating 250 in the dining room, providing quick service for 25, and a bar serving 50. The grill, delivery, food preparation, and cooking services are all carefully considered.

Within the limitations of the lots, many different arrangements of facilities and services are possible, and these have been tried out in schematic plan diagrams to show the possible maximum number of customers that can be accommodated at tables, counter, and bar. Such an analysis is extremely important to a restaurant owner, for maximum seating without crowding means maximum profit.

A preliminary diagrammatic analysis of this kind is a distinct contribution on the part of the architect to the success of the restaurant. For that matter, it would be equally desirable in connection with any other type of building, for it gives the owner an opportunity to analyze his operational problems and possible financial returns to choose the best scheme, and to proceed with confidence.

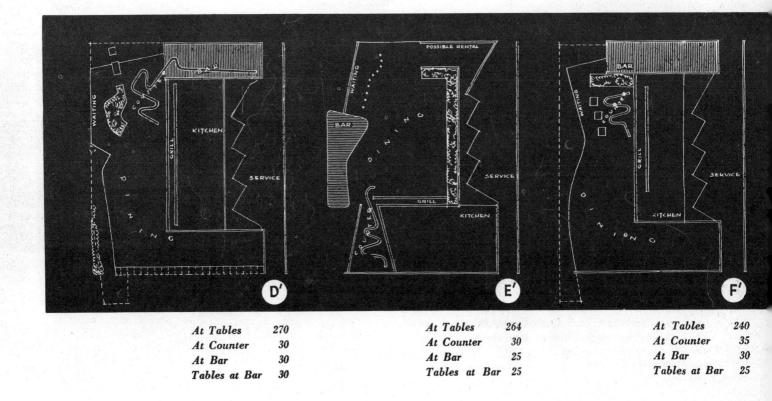

	D'		E'		F'
At Tables	270	At Tables	264	At Tables	240
At Counter	30	At Counter	30	At Counter	35
At Bar	30	At Bar	25	At Bar	30
Tables at Bar	30	Tables at Bar	25	Tables at Bar	25

FOR PLANE PASSENGERS AND PERSONNEL

Two Airport Restaurants for Sky Chefs, Inc.

J. Gordon Carr, Architect

BEGINNING its career just a month before Pearl Harbor, Sky Chefs, Inc., has been carried aloft with increasing air traffic until it now comprises a chain of a score of airport restaurants. Construction and design have hardly known anything but wartime conditions, but occasionally the operations have been blessed with priorities, so important were eating facilities to air travelers. Designwise, the earlier units were born with the benefit of architectural attention; Mr. Carr got them started by doing

the first two or three, and by designing trade mark, china and tableware, uniforms, menus, color schemes and such.

Starting in crowded quarters, with strong emphasis on counter service, the restaurants have shown trends mentioned in ARCHITECTURAL RECORD's Airport issue of last April, notably the encouragement of airport visitors who may be but casually interested in flying. Later restaurants show a separation of the counter from the main dining room, the former serving mainly airport personnel, the latter designed for family custom. These restaurants give a third type of service—meals for in-flight plane passengers. It is interesting to note that this service, contracted for by the airlines, amounts to about half the business; the counter service for about 45 per cent. In wartime

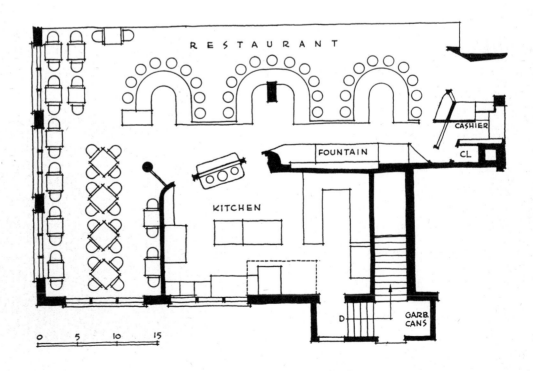

Hartford unit of Sky Chefs, Inc., an example of coordinated design where the architect's control extended even to tableware

the family-type portion has been held down, but is expected to develop importantly when the family car attains full usefulness.

The unit on the preceding page is one of the early ones, at busy El Paso Airport; the one on this page is Hartford, Conn., also one of the first smaller units.

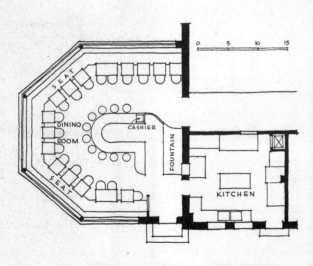

Ezra Stoller

INDEX

WIDENER COLLEGE
LIBRARY
CHESTER, PENNSYLVANIA